USA TODAY

Lifeline

BIOGRAPHIES

BILL GATES
Entrepreneur and Philanthropist

by Jeanne M. Lesinski

Twenty-First Century Books · Minneapolis

To my mother, who helped me buy my first computer

Twenty-First Century Books
A division of Lerner Publishing Group, Inc.
241 First Avenue North
Minneapolis, MN 55401 U.S.A.

Website address: www.lernerbooks.com

The publisher wishes to thank Richard Curtis, Nancy Blair, and Ben Nussbaum of USA TODAY for their help in preparing this book.

Library of Congress Cataloging-in-Publication Data

Lesinski, Jeanne M.
    Bill Gates : entrepreneur and philanthropist / by Jeanne M. Lesinski
        p.m.   c.m. — (Lifeline biographies)
    Includes bibliographical references and index.
    978-1-58013-570-2 (lib. bdg. : alk. paper)
    1. Gates, Bill, 1955—Juvenile literature. 2. Businesspeople—United States—Biography—Juvenile literature. 3. Computer software industry—United States—Juvenile literature. 4. Microsoft Corporation—History—Juvenile literature. I. Title.
HD9696.63.U62G374 2009
338.7'610053092—dc22   2008008565

Manufactured in the United States of America
1 2 3 4 5 6 – PA – 14 13 12 11 10 09

World stage: Bill Gates is all smiles as he attends a media conference at the World Economic Forum in Switzerland in 2008. Gates spoke to business and government leaders at the forum.

Microsoft Mogul

Billionaire computer tycoon. Ruthless competitor. Astute predictor of future technology. Lucky.

People have described Bill Gates in many ways. But he is more than just one of the world's richest men and cofounder of Microsoft Corporation. Through his charitable organization, the Bill & Melinda Gates Foundation, Gates is also one of the world's most generous givers, donating hundreds of millions of dollars to people around the globe. The foundation grew even larger in 2006 when investor Warren Buffett pledged to donate much of his vast wealth to the charity. The billions of dollars Buffett has promised would be the largest philanthropic gift in history.

In the United States, Gates focuses his charity work on education and has helped students from all walks of life receive vital training for the future. Many public libraries in the United States, for example, receive funding from the Bill & Melinda Gates Foundation for computer upgrades and access to new information technology. Overseas, the foundation promotes agricultural and financial programs and is dedicated to stopping the worldwide AIDS epidemic as well as other deadly diseases.

Despite Gates's focus on his foundation work and on family life, he is still helping to lead the computer industry into the future. Microsoft spends billions of dollars each year on research and development. With products such as the video game system Xbox 360 and Windows

Video game revolution: The Xbox 360 is one of the hottest video game consoles on the market.

Vista, the company continues to lead the computer industry in new and exciting directions. Microsoft also invests heavily in technologies that were created by others.

When Gates left college in 1975 to focus on the newly founded Microsoft Corporation, many people close to him tried to talk him out of it. Opening and running a new business is difficult and uncertain work. Yet in the years since then, this unassuming man has built a company from two employees to more than thirty thousand. He has led a far-reaching technological revolution, becoming one of the most influential— and philanthropic— business leaders in the world.

USA TODAY Snapshots®

Entrepreneurs wanted

Forty-seven percent of Americans dream of owning a business. Whose career they would most like to have:

Bill Gates (Microsoft) **32%**

Oprah Winfrey (Harpo) **15%**

Ben Cohen/Jerry Greenfield (Ben and Jerry's Ice Cream) **15%**

Martha Stewart (Martha Stewart Living Omnimedia) **8%**

Ralph Lauren (Polo and Ralph Lauren) **6%**

Source: Survey conducted by Harris Interactive for lawyers.com of 1,014 Americans

By Darryl Haralson and Marcy E. Mullins, USA TODAY, 2002

Seattle: This image of downtown Seattle was taken in 1962. Bill's parents raised their children in the View Ridge neighborhood of the city.

Young Thinker

After serving in the army in World War II (1939–1945), Bill Gates's father, William Gates Sr., studied law at the University of Washington in Seattle. There, he fell in love with a charming and energetic education student, Mary Maxwell. The two married in 1951 and settled in the View Ridge neighborhood in Seattle. William, who went by the name Bill, joined a law firm in Seattle. Mary taught at area schools.

The couple's first child was born in 1953, a daughter named Kristianne. Two years later, on October 28, 1955, William Henry Gates III joined the family. His younger sister, Libby, was born in 1964.

Right away, Little Bill, as he was called, demonstrated good humor and high energy, rocking in his cradle. Later, he grew particularly fond of a rocking horse, which he would ride for hours. Little Bill discovered that rocking improved his ability to think—and think he did.

At school Bill was the youngest student in his class. Though he was small for his age

Mother's helper: Mary Gates often brought Bill along when she made presentations at various schools in Seattle.

and somewhat clumsy, he shined academically. Certain subjects, such as math and science, were easy for him. Bill read voraciously. He read entire textbooks in the first few days of class. He entered and won summer reading contests at the local public library.

 Bill has rocked back and forth since he was a tiny child. His mother believed it helped calm him. Bill believes it helps him concentrate.

At the age of eight, Bill started to read the 1960 edition of *The World Book Encyclopedia.* "I was determined to read straight through every volume," he recalled. By the time he reached the entries under the letter *P*, Bill discovered a more detailed encyclopedia and decided he would never have enough time or patience to read the entire new set.

Mary Gates recalled that her son was always thinking. "He'd never ever be ready when we were going someplace, and we'd call out to him, 'What are you doing?' Bill would answer, 'Thinking.'" Bill even chided his parents, asking, "Don't you ever think?"

Father figure: Bill's father William Gates II, shown here in the mid-1990s, was a lawyer.

"We didn't have a good answer to that," Bill Gates Sr. added. "We weren't sure we ever did."

Intelligent and energetic, Mary Gates worked with volunteer organizations in her community and rose to national leadership positions. Since Mary was so busy, her mother, Adelle Maxwell (nicknamed "Gam"), cared for the grandchildren after school. When Bill and his sisters came home from school, Gam met them with snacks and activities. Weeknight television was not allowed, but reading and games were household staples. Board games, puzzles, and card games went on for hours. Gam loved card games and taught the children to play bridge. She nicknamed Bill "Trey," after the cardplayer term for "three" and because he was William Henry Gates III.

Bill Gates Sr. recalled that after dinner on Sundays, the entire family would gather to play games. "The play was quite serious. Winning mattered," Bill's father remembered. Fiercely competitive, Trey didn't like to lose.

> **i** At around the age of ten, Bill marked "scientist" on a survey that asked him what he wanted to be when he was older.

Looking for a Challenge

When Bill was in fourth grade, the family moved to a new home in the Laurelhurst area of Seattle. By this time, Bill was bored with school. He applied himself in the subjects he liked—math and reading—but made little effort at those that he found boring. Left-handed, Bill sometimes took notes with his right hand, just to give himself a little challenge when bored in class.

At the Laurelhurst Elementary School library, Bill worked to find wrongly shelved and lost books, a job that demonstrated his diligence and attention to detail. Sometimes the teachers had to make him stop working and go out for recess. In the library, Bill discovered the work of Leonardo da Vinci, a scientist and artist who lived in Italy from 1452 to 1519. When asked about his future career, Bill answered that he wanted to be a scientist.

At times, people thought Bill was a goof-off or class clown because he didn't seem to pay attention in school. He would make wisecracks and sometimes argue with teachers. His parents thought he was a dramatic underachiever. They wanted him to respect the educational process.

Bill was not interested in team sports. He tried Little League baseball, but the pace was too slow for him. He found roller-skating, tennis, and skiing—both on snow and water—to be more exciting.

September 19, 2000

Discoveries were Leonardo's true masterpieces

From the Pages of
USA TODAY

In his forceful new biography, British science writer Michael White accomplishes the impossible: He makes Leonardo da Vinci's work as a painter beside the point.

White, a former science editor for British *GQ* and professor at Oxford's d'Overbroeck's College, deftly leads readers through the remarkable machinations of a man who had, in his words, "an almost psychotic need to discover, to unravel the mystery of life." Across a roster of disciplines, from anatomy to optics to warfare, Leonardo managed to get there first—to make discoveries that would take others hundreds of years to replicate.

During his lifetime, Leonardo (1452–1519) compiled more than 13,000 manuscript pages and thousands of intricate drawings to illustrate his observations and experiments. Using excerpts from these, White argues that Leonardo "worked with scientific precision centuries ahead of his time." Leonardo saw, for example, light and sound as behaving in a similar way.

"He of course had no idea of the electromagnetic spectrum or concepts such as frequency or amplitude, but he clearly saw that light and sound may travel through a medium by what he described as a 'tremor,'" White writes, quoting from Leonardo's notebooks. His observations predated those of Christian Huygens, who published his theory of the wavelike nature of light in 1690.

Similarly, Leonardo experimented with a prism, splitting the components of white light into its constituent parts. He placed a glass of water on a windowsill so the sun's rays would create a rainbow. Isaac Newton famously re-created the experiment in the 1660s. Leonardo was equally successful as a military engineer, coming up with designs for a parachute, mechanized vehicles, pumps and digging machines that were essentially rediscovered hundreds of years later.

While Leonardo will probably remain better known for the *Mona Lisa* than the early submarine, White makes a good case for why he ought to be equally, or perhaps more, celebrated for his scientific prowess.

—Dina Temple-Raston, September 19, 2000

In summer he hung out at the Laurelhurst Beach Club, where he could swim, dive, and sail on Lake Washington. The family rented rustic cabins on the Hood Canal near Puget Sound. There, they would gather with friends for picnics, games, and campfires. Bill also joined a Boy Scout troop, where fun was foremost and formality nowhere to be found. With its hiking and camping trips, the troop fed Bill's craving for adventure.

The Gates family regularly went to services at the University Congregational Church. When challenged by the church pastor to memorize the Sermon on the Mount, Bill flawlessly recited this lengthy passage from the Bible. For his effort, he won a free dinner at the Space Needle, a famous Seattle landmark, compliments of the pastor.

Gatesway Incorporated

During sixth grade, Bill still lacked a focus for his intellect. "My desk was always messy, and I didn't seem to be paying attention. I was always out there on the playground trying to form some sort of group of guys, or sort of laughing about something when you weren't supposed to be laughing," he remembered. Bill did find satisfaction with one school group, the Century Club, made up of bright sixth graders. With the Century Club, Bill went on educational field trips, played board games, and discussed books and current events.

He did well in a special economics class at school. For the class, he created a fictitious business report called "Invest with Gatesway Incorporated." Bill imagined himself as a young inventor who manufactured and marketed a new product.

Bill and Mary Gates became concerned about their son when he was ready for junior high. "He was so small and shy, in need of protection, and his interests were so very different from the typical sixth grader's," his father remembered. The Gateses debated whether or not to send their underachieving son to a private school, where class sizes would be smaller and discipline more stringent. They wanted their son to learn good study habits. They wanted him to prepare for college

Junior high: As an eighth grader, Bill *(left)* was smaller than many of his peers.

and a career. Finally, they decided to send Bill to Lakeside School, an exclusive boys' school in Seattle for students in grades seven through twelve. There students wore jackets and neckties, carried briefcases, and had assigned seating—even at lunch.

The first year, 1967, Bill tried to adjust to his new school and schoolmates. He still didn't work hard. He was a B student, except in honors algebra, in which he earned an A minus. He hung out with other students interested in math and science. As usual, he read a lot, including biographies of the French emperor Napoléon Bonaparte and U.S. president Franklin D. Roosevelt.

Budding Interest

When Bill and the other students started math and science classes in 1968, they discovered an intriguing new machine in Lakeside's McAlister Hall. It was a Teletype machine, made up of a keyboard, a printer, and a paper-tape punch and reader. The machine could be hooked up to a telephone by placing the receiver in a special cradle. Through the telephone lines, the Teletype machine communicated with a computer at a local General Electric office.

IN FOCUS

The Teletype

In 1844 the inventor Samuel F. B. Morse created the telegraph. The telegraph sent information across great distances through a wire and was extremely helpful. One problem with the design was that operators had to be at each end of the wire to send and receive the information. Many people thought it would be a good idea to create a device that would type the incoming messages and allow messages to be sent without someone waiting to write them down. The idea for a new machine eventually became the Teletype.

The first few designs of the Teletype were very complicated. The machines were connected to one another through telegraph lines. They had to be linked perfectly to send messages correctly. By the 1910s, the first successful Teletypes were being used. Within the next twenty years, Teletypes became in important communication tool. But by the 1970s,

Old technology: These Teletype machines were made in 1962.

when Bill and his friends at Lakeside began working with Teletypes, they were becoming old technology.

At this time, in the late 1960s, personal computers had not yet been invented. Instead, businesses and universities used mainframe computers that were bigger than refrigerators. Holes punched in paper tapes instructed the computers to perform mathematical calculations and other tasks. Researchers at universities and laboratories used the computers to analyze data. Businesses, such as electric companies, used computers to calculate and print monthly bills for customers.

Mainframe computers cost many millions of dollars, so many businesses and universities often shared a single mainframe. Users at different locations made paper tapes carrying instructions. Using Teletype machines and telephone lines, users sent the instructions to the mainframe computer they shared with others.

Massive mainframe: A technician makes an adjustment to a mainframe computer in the mid-1970s.

At first the Lakeside students did not know a thing about computers—and their teachers didn't know much more. But, like a complex puzzle, the computer gave feedback and information. If the user correctly wrote instructions, called programs, the computer responded with solutions to mathematical questions. If a program wasn't written correctly, it couldn't produce useful responses.

To Bill the computer was a challenge to be mastered. Describing his first encounter with the computer, Bill recalled, "I wrote my first . . .

program when I was thirteen years old. It was for playing tic-tac-toe. The computer I used was huge and cumbersome and slow and absolutely compelling." Bill had found his focus.

Since the school had no formal course in computing, teachers and students alike taught themselves from computer manuals. Bill and other students spent as much time as they could using the computer. They learned different programming languages, each with its own particular rules and vocabulary. These languages included BASIC— Beginner's All-purpose Symbolic Instruction Code—and FORTRAN, a programming language used by scientists.

The students wrote simple programs—also called software—which grew in size and complexity. Bill wrote a program to play the game

Early years: Bill looks on as classmate Paul Allen uses a Teletype machine at Lakeside School in 1968. Bill's and Paul's interest in computers led them to become friends and business partners.

Risk using a computer. In this game, players pretend to take over the world. Another student wrote a program to calculate grade point averages using the computer.

Bill worked in the computer room so much that some other students complained that he was hogging the equipment. These same students often came to Bill for answers when they got stuck with programming problems.

In ninth grade, Bill's school performance changed dramatically. "I came up with a new form of rebellion," he explained. "I hadn't been getting good grades, but I decided to get all As without taking a book home. I didn't go to math class, because I knew enough and had read ahead, and I placed within the top ten people in the nation on an aptitude exam. That established my independence and taught me I didn't need to rebel anymore." Bill became a straight-A student.

At home his room was a jumble of paper computer tapes, dirty clothes, and reading material. After trying various ploys to get Bill to clean his room, his parents decided to close the door on the mess.

Paying His Way

General Electric charged the Lakeside students eighty-nine dollars per month for the Teletype and eight dollars an hour for computer time. At these rates, the computer students quickly racked up enormous bills. The Lakeside Mothers' Club helped fund their computer use through an annual garage sale, but the students needed to find other ways to pay for computer time.

While Bill's parents paid his school tuition and bought his books, they insisted he pay for his own computer fees. "This is what drove me to the commercial side of the software business," Bill explained. He wanted to work with computers and get paid for it.

Another influence was Bill's best friend, Kent Evans. Kent was very interested in both computers and the business world, and he exuded confidence that was unusual for someone his age. For a time, he and

Bill were inseparable. "We read *Fortune* [business magazine] together; we were going to conquer the world," Bill said.

The Lakeside computer students were elated when Computer Center Corporation opened its business in Seattle. The company owned a mainframe computer, and the Lakeside students hooked up to it using a Teletype machine and phone lines. Because so few people understood computers in those years, the company director decided to rely on the Lakeside students for help.

The students worked during the company's off-hours, testing the computer and fixing bugs or flaws in the programs. Students caught buses from Lakeside to "C-Cubed" (as the company was soon dubbed for the three Cs in its title) and stayed there for hours. Sometimes Bill sneaked out of his room at night to go work on the computer. If he missed the last bus, he'd have to walk 3 miles (5 kilometers) home.

Eventually C-Cubed went out of business. Undeterred, Bill and some other students, among them upperclassman Paul Allen, found weekend

IN FOCUS

Hacking the System

The students of Lakeside were allowed free access to the C-Cubed computer. The company told them to find ways to crash the system. The company hoped to learn from each crash and improve its system.

Bill, Paul Allen, and others found a way to break into the accounting system at C-Cubed. They got passwords and changed how much computer-use time they were being billed for. The company found out about their experiment and developed a new security system. The company asked the students to break it. It took the students only a half hour. Even so, the company fined the students for changing their bills and banned the students from using the system for an entire summer.

and summer jobs writing programs for other computer companies. Computer programs are written in steps. The first step is to develop the process for solving a problem. The next step is to write "code"—a program that will solve the problem. Gates and Allen wrote computer code in return for free computer time as well as for payment.

Bill also took a job with a company that was analyzing traffic patterns. Using hoses laid across highways, the company collected data about traffic use. Bill took charge of counting the data and putting it into a computer at the University of Washington. He hired several Lakeside students to help count, while he input the data by punched tape. Then he printed out the results.

Tragedy and Opportunity

During Bill's junior year, Lakeside merged with Saint Nicholas, an all-girls' school. With more students—about five hundred—the class schedule was difficult to determine by hand. Each of the students attended eight classes a day. Some classes met only one day a week. Some classes included an extra two-hour laboratory period.

Several teachers tried to write a computer program to create the schedule, but they couldn't do it on their own. They tapped Bill and his friend Kent Evans for help. The two boys spent long hours at the task, often going without much-needed sleep. As the deadline neared, disaster struck. Kent fell to his death in a mountaineering accident.

Bill was devastated. "I had never thought of people dying," he remembers. He was supposed to speak at Kent's memorial service, but he was too upset to do so. "For two weeks I couldn't do anything at all," Bill wrote. After some time, Bill continued to work on the scheduling program. He and Paul Allen eventually finished it.

During Bill's senior year, he and Paul, who had already graduated, took programming jobs with the engineering firm TRW in Vancouver, Washington. The company was writing a computer program that would control the Bonneville Power Administration's electricity distribution grid. School officials gave Bill permission to miss classes so he could

Taking it easy: Bill relaxes in Lakeside's computer room. A Teletype machine is shown in the lower left corner.

attend work. The job was considered his senior project.

The duo also tried to build their own special-purpose computer and software. Computer chips—the brains of a computer—were very primitive during this time, so Gates and Allen tried to think of a simple job for their machine. They came up with Traf-O-Data, a system to count and analyze traffic patterns.

Although they were never able to finish the project, their friendship grew as they worked together. "I was lucky in my early teens to become friends with Paul Allen," Bill once remarked. "Paul had lots of answers to things I was curious about.... I was more of a math person than Paul, and I understood software better than anyone he knew. We were interactive resources for each other. We asked or answered questions, drew diagrams, or brought each other's attention to related information. We liked to challenge each other."

Bill went to his senior prom dressed in a white coat, a pink shirt with ruffles, and a top hat. He even carried a fancy walking stick.

Bill's life didn't revolve solely around computing, however. In the summer of 1972, before his senior year, he worked as a congressional page in Washington, D.C. By this time, Bill the shy young man had grown confident. He had starred in three school plays. He aggressively played chess and a Japanese game of strategy called Go. He drove his family's red Mustang convertible, water-skied, and went to the senior prom. He also grew closer to his mother, with whom he had frequently argued.

As to life after high school, Bill knew he had lots of options. He had good grades and test scores. On the SAT, he scored 800 (a perfect score) on the math portion and 790 on the verbal portion. He won a National Merit Scholarship. After making a quick tour of East Coast colleges, Bill applied to Harvard, Yale, and Princeton. He was accepted at all three and chose to attend Harvard.

USA TODAY Snapshots®

Seattle is best-educated big city

Large cities with the highest percentage of residents age 25 and older with at least a bachelor's degree:

City	Percentage
Seattle	48.8%
Raleigh, N.C.	48%
San Francisco	47.8%
Washington	42.5%
Atlanta	41.2%
Austin	40.6%

Source: U.S. Census Bureau   By Bob Laird, USA TODAY, 2004

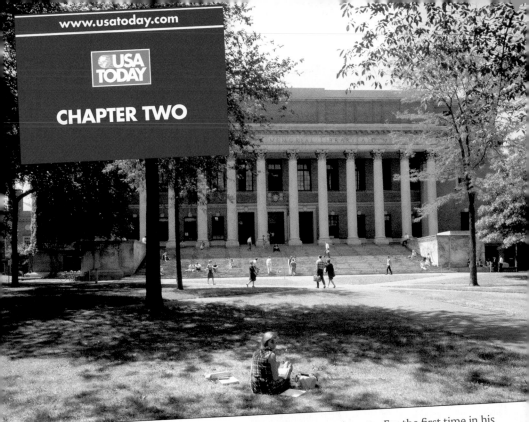

Harvard bound: Bill attended Harvard University in Massachusetts. For the first time in his life, Bill found he wasn't the smartest student in class.

Finding Focus

Harvard University, located in Cambridge, Massachusetts, near Boston, provided the intense intellectual experience eighteen-year-old Bill Gates craved. During his freshman year, in 1973, he studied advanced math, Greek literature, English, social science, and organic chemistry. He often skipped the classes in which he was enrolled and attended other classes just for fun. He used the university's computers and continued working on his Traf-O-Data project.

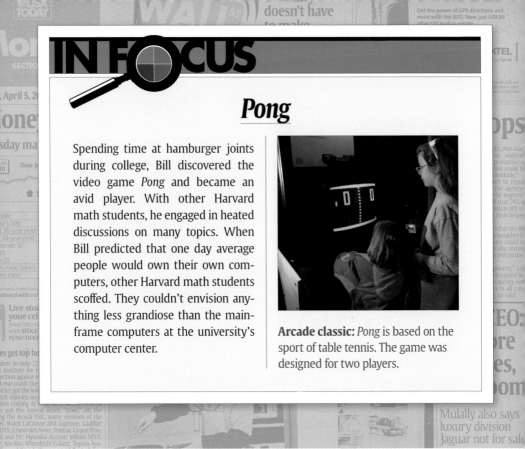

IN FOCUS

Pong

Spending time at hamburger joints during college, Bill discovered the video game *Pong* and became an avid player. With other Harvard math students, he engaged in heated discussions on many topics. When Bill predicted that one day average people would own their own computers, other Harvard math students scoffed. They couldn't envision anything less grandiose than the mainframe computers at the university's computer center.

Arcade classic: *Pong* is based on the sport of table tennis. The game was designed for two players.

Attending Harvard, Bill learned that he was no longer the smartest student in math class. The experience humbled Bill, who had planned to major in math. Instead, he considered majoring in law or one of the sciences. He also considered taking time off from college and getting a job. He interviewed with several companies.

During his sophomore year, Bill met a math and science student named Steve Ballmer, who lived in the same residence hall. The outgoing and charming Ballmer made sure that Bill had a life outside of his studies. The friends played the video game Breakout and attended all-night poker games in the dormitory. "He'd play poker until six in the morning, then I'd run into him at breakfast and discuss applied mathematics," Ballmer recalled. Together Gates and Ballmer took graduate-level courses in math and economics.

Meanwhile, Paul Allen had accepted a job near Boston, and he and Bill stayed close friends. Realizing that their traffic analyzing machine was not going to make it to market, they decided to focus on computer programs instead of hardware, the physical parts of computers. They talked for many hours about possible software projects. They also kept up on the computer industry's latest developments in computer-chip technology.

Altair Leads the Way

The January 1975 issue of *Popular Electronics* featured an article on the Altair 8800, the first personal computer—a small computer that fits on a desk—for sale to the public. The computer didn't look like much, just a rectangular box with several rows of little lights and several more rows of tiny toggle switches across the front. It had no keyboard and no disk drive—none of the parts that would later become standard on personal computers. And the buyer had to assemble the Altair 8800 from a kit. Only people who were very interested in electronics bought this early machine.

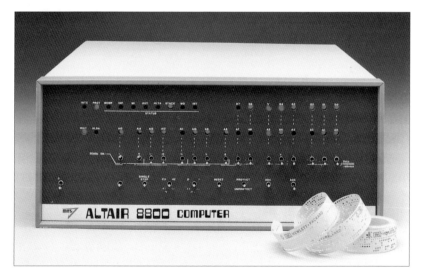

Early computer: The Altair 8800 printed data on punch tape *(bottom right)*.

No matter how primitive it was, the Altair 8800 was a computer, and it needed software. Gates and Allen decided to write a program that would enable the Altair to run other programs such as BASIC. They hoped to sell the program to the Altair's manufacturer, Micro Instrumentation and Telemetry System (MITS), in Albuquerque, New Mexico.

For six weeks, Bill almost lived at the Harvard computer center— that is, when he wasn't at class, grabbing a meal, or playing poker. He could nap almost anywhere and did, even in a corner of the computer lab or slumped over a keyboard. Allen came to the center when he was off work. As they neared the end of the project, Gates and Allen hired several other Harvard students to write small portions of their BASIC program. As the two had hoped, Ed Roberts, the creator of the Altair, agreed to buy the rights to use the program, called MS-BASIC, in his computers. Afterward, Gates and Allen still had to fix dozens of bugs in the program.

In the spring of 1975, as Bill finished his classes at Harvard, he debated whether or not to return in the fall. Paul Allen had accepted a job with MITS as its director of software. Bill realized that he was poised at a pivotal point in a technological revolution.

BASIC Beginning

For decades, people at businesses, schools, laboratories, and in government had used adding machines to calculate sums from handwritten ledgers. They had typed documents, including whole books, page by page on typewriters. If a typist needed more than one copy of a document, he or she placed carbon paper between sheets of typing paper. Making changes and correcting errors were time consuming and expensive.

Bill could see that with a personal computer, calculating, typing, making multiple copies, and other business and school tasks would be easier. Bill wanted to help solve millions of people's everyday problems and make money in the process.

USA TODAY

Money

SECTION B

June 22, 1999

Microprocessors have upgraded the way we live

<u>From the Pages of USA TODAY</u>

In 1999 Bill Gates wrote an essay for USA TODAY. The following is an excerpt.

I was in high school when I first read about the microprocessor, in an article my friend Paul Allen found in *Electronics* magazine. Paul and I already wrote software, but that article got us thinking that we might be able to make money doing it.

Then, there weren't any pure software companies. Computer makers, such as IBM and Digital, wrote their own proprietary software for their own machines. They certainly didn't want Paul or me writing it for them.

Intel's microprocessor changed all that. First, Intel didn't make computers or software. Yet to do anything useful, its new chip needed software. So Paul and I saw a chance to start a software company. Second, it was clear that the microprocessor would dramatically change the computer industry by cutting manufacturing costs and adding new features. Intel's advertisement for its new chip, "Announcing a new era of integrated electronics," proved very far-sighted.

He decided to take a leave of absence from Harvard to start a software company with Paul Allen. Bill's parents did not agree with his decision and tried to talk him out of it. Though Bill did go back to Harvard for a semester or two, in the end, his software business won out.

In 1977 Bill Gates left Harvard for Albuquerque on what became a permanent leave of absence. Paul Allen had quit MITS in 1976. He and Bill formed a legal partnership and registered the name Microsoft

When Intel's Ted Hoff (with Federico Faggin and Stan Mazor) invented the microprocessor, he didn't intend to change the world. Asked by one of Intel's customers to produce a dozen custom chips for a range of calculators, Hoff thought it would be easier to manufacture a general-purpose chip that would rely on software to make it perform different tasks. The result was the Intel 4004 microprocessor. Built on a sliver of silicon, it contained 2,300 tiny transistors and was effectively a computer on a single chip. Introduced in 1971, it launched an entire industry.

It also changed my life, with the help of what claimed to be the "World's First Minicomputer Kit"—the MITS Altair 8800. Named after a world in the movie *Forbidden Planet*, the 1975 Altair used an Intel 8080 microprocessor and cost under $400. But it couldn't do anything useful. It had no keyboard or screen—and no software.

So Paul and I formed a partnership we called Micro-soft and wrote some software that would make the Altair perform simple tasks.

Six years later, when IBM launched the first modern PC, we supplied operating system software for that, too.

Powered by the microprocessor, the PC has revolutionized how we collect, store and use information, how we communicate, how we work, learn and play.

Today's PCs, using sophisticated software and microprocessors containing more than 9 million transistors, give even a child access to more computing power than an old mainframe computer.

It's remarkable how we now take all that power for granted. Using a basic home PC costing less than $1,000, you can balance your household budget, do your taxes, write letters to friends and fax or e-mail them over the Internet, listen to CDs or the radio, watch the news, consult a doctor, play games, book a vacation, view a house, buy a book or a car. . . . The list is endless.

—Bill Gates, June 22, 1999

with the state of New Mexico. They were in business.

But what kind of business could thrive in a hacker climate? Back then computer hackers were people so interested in computers that they would give away their own programs for free. And they were not above copying other people's programs. Bill had caused a stir in 1975 when he wrote a letter in the *Computer Notes* newsletter. He said that computer users were stealing if they copied rather than bought

Microsoft's first home: Microsoft had its first offices in this Albuquerque, New Mexico, office building from September 1976 to December 1978.

computer programs. Bill argued that software programs were "intellectual property," meaning that they should be legally protected through copyrights, like books. Because of Bill's efforts, copying computer programs became illegal.

Soon companies such as Apple, Commodore, and Radio Shack got into the personal computer business. As computer makers developed more powerful chips, software programs became more powerful too. The new programs could perform more complicated operations. Word-processing programs, for example, allowed users to move words and paragraphs around in typed documents. They could produce different styles and sizes of type. Other programs could show and manipulate graphic images. And the programs could perform all of these tasks faster than ever before.

Although Gates and Allen had sold the rights to MS-BASIC to MITS, they were able to get the rights back legally, without payment. At Microsoft they wrote BASIC programs to run the various new computers on the market. Each brand of computer was just different enough from the others that it needed its own customized BASIC program.

Bill quickly saw that most people who were using the BASIC program hadn't bothered to buy the software. They were simply copying it. One estimate said only 10 percent of users owned the software legally.

Microsoft sold its BASIC program for a very low price. Bill believed that so many people would eventually buy the program that the company would make a profit, even with the low price. Microsoft's motto was "A computer on every desk and in every home."

USA TODAY Snapshots®

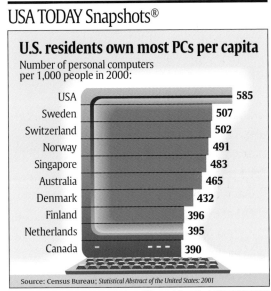

U.S. residents own most PCs per capita

Number of personal computers per 1,000 people in 2000:

USA	585
Sweden	507
Switzerland	502
Norway	491
Singapore	483
Australia	465
Denmark	432
Finland	396
Netherlands	395
Canada	390

Source: Census Bureau; *Statistical Abstract of the United States: 2001*

By Amy Cohen and Sam Ward, USA TODAY, 2002

Doing It His Way

Though Bill could probably have gotten money from his family to help start his business, he didn't want it. He wanted Microsoft to support itself from the beginning. For three years, he worked long hours, often sixteen-hour days. He wrote computer code and handled the business end of the company. He made sales calls to such companies as General Electric, National Cash Register, and Citibank. These big companies needed software for their mainframes and other computers. He also talked with computer makers about selling MS-BASIC and other programming languages with their machines.

Though he was now in his early twenties, Bill's slight build, unruly hair, and freckles made him look like a teenager. His youthful looks sometimes gave potential buyers pause. But as soon as buyers heard him talk about his company's products, they could tell that he knew the business. As Microsoft sold more programs, Bill hired more employees. Many were old friends from Lakeside School.

When the new employees arrived at work, they found a place that was more like a college than a business. There

First product: Bill *(right)* and Paul Allen *(left)* show off some of their first software disks. The disks are sitting near the computer's keyboard.

was no dress code—programmers wore jeans. They hung posters on the walls and listened to rock music if they wanted. The company gave out free sodas. Some programmers arrived in the afternoon and worked until evening. Then they grabbed a bite to eat, maybe went to a movie, and came back to work a late-night session. They straggled home in the early morning hours, returning to work again around noon.

Despite the relaxed atmosphere, the programmers took their jobs seriously—as though they were on a mission. They were going

High speed: The Albuquerque police took this photograph of Bill in 1977 after a traffic violation.

to change the world. But exactly how much and in what ways wouldn't become clear until some years later.

No one at Microsoft worked harder than Bill Gates. He was so preoccupied with his work that he often forgot to tend to his appearance or eat meals. Sometimes, when his secretary came to work in the morning, she found her boss asleep on the floor of his office.

Even though he worked very hard, Bill needed to relax too. He went to movies. He bought a used sports car and took high-speed nighttime drives in the desert around Albuquerque. He racked up speeding tickets. At least once, Paul Allen had to bail him out of jail when he forgot his driver's license.

A Big Move

Microsoft no longer had ties to MITS, and it was often difficult to convince programmers to move to Albuquerque, which was far from most major universities and big cities. So, in 1979 Bill decided to move the company, which then numbered a dozen employees. Although most computer companies were located in California, Gates's ties to his family were strong. He opted to move Microsoft to Bellevue, Washington, near Seattle.

Bill knew that to be truly successful, Microsoft needed to sell more than just language products like BASIC. It needed to sell word-processing and operating system software. Bill believed that personal computers would become essential for businesses. He predicted that many people would want a computer at home.

Bill also realized that Microsoft needed more efficient business practices. Bill knew that his college friend Steve Ballmer, with his business experience and social skills, would be a great asset, even though he knew little about computers. As it turned out, Ballmer was available. He became Bill's assistant and one of the company's best promoters.

MS-DOS for IBM

In 1980 IBM (International Business Machines), then the leading manufacturer of mainframe computers, decided to get into the personal computer business. Because IBM executives wanted a product ready for sale in a short time, they decided not to build their own computer from scratch. Instead, they would build a computer using parts that were already being made by other manufacturers. And instead of writing their own software for the IBM personal computer (PC), they contacted Microsoft.

First personal computer: This man is trying out the personal computer that IBM unveiled in 1983. IBM asked Microsoft to write software for their PCs.

Twenty-five-year-old Bill Gates agreed to provide IBM with a group of software programs, including a disk operating system. The operating system, or OS, is the master program that runs the computer. It controls the keyboard, monitor, and information storage system.

To get a head start on writing an operating system for IBM, Bill bought one from Seattle Computer Products. For a year, nearly half of the sixty employees at Microsoft worked day and night on the IBM project. They adapted the OS for the IBM machine and named it MS-DOS.

Because IBM had used off-the-shelf parts to build its PC, other computer makers could build similar computers, which came to be called clones. The clones needed software too, and Bill was right there, offering MS-DOS and other products. Royalties began to pour in from PC makers everywhere. Eventually MS-DOS became the standard operating system for IBM PCs and clones (only Apple brand computers

IN FOCUS

The Big Apple

One of the most important U.S. computer companies at this time was Apple. Steve Wozniak and Steve Jobs had started the company in 1975. They released the Apple 1 computer in 1976. To make its computers easy to use, Apple introduced a system called the graphical user interface, or GUI (pronounced "GOO-ee"). The GUI system involved a device called a mouse.

Apple users used the mouse to point at small pictures on the screen to control their computers. They didn't have to remember complicated word and number commands as a user did with MS-DOS.

Bill Gates was watching what Apple was doing. He could see that making computers easier to use was an important step. He believed that GUI was the key.

> **ⓘ** Bill licensed MS-DOS to IBM on a royalty basis, meaning that for each copy of the system sold, IBM would pay a percentage of the money to Microsoft. When IBM introduced its personal computer in 1981, buyers snapped it up. Royalties from IBM began to pour into Microsoft.

used their own operating system). All the computer users who were using MS-DOS could share files and documents.

By the end of 1982, Microsoft had sold $32 million in software. It had about two hundred employees, but it soon lost a very important

Computer boom: Bill poses in front of a variety of computers that were available in the early 1980s.

Friend and cohort: Paul Allen in his Microsoft office. Bill and Allen have been friends and business partners since their school days.

one. Paul Allen learned that he had Hodgkin's disease, a treatable form of cancer, and left Microsoft in early 1983 to focus on other goals—playing in a rock band was one of them. Though Bill felt his friend's absence, he had a company to run. Microsoft depended on him for leadership—to decide what products to make and how to sell them. The stress kept Bill up at night with insomnia.

 Bill Gates was a multimillionaire before he turned thirty years old.

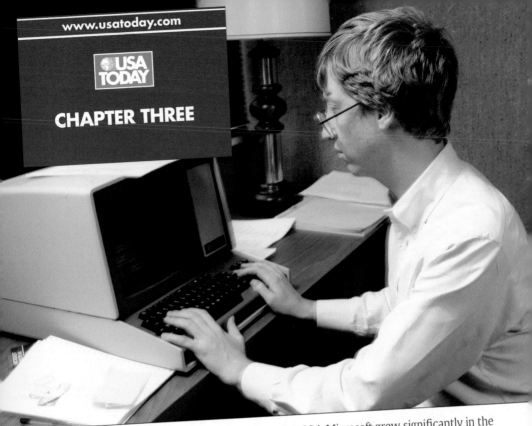

Computing success: Bill works on a computer in 1984. Microsoft grew significantly in the 1980s.

Windows of Opportunity

During the 1980s, Bill focused Microsoft on two areas: developing products for individual computer users and creating an international sales force. He added a customer service department. Microsoft grew dramatically.

In 1982 Microsoft introduced a spreadsheet program called Multiplan. It allowed businesspeople to perform accounting and other

New product: This was the first logo for Microsoft's Multiplan spreadsheet software.

financial calculations. The next year, Microsoft came out with Word, a word-processing program featuring WYSIWYG (pronounced "wizzy-wig"), which stands for "What You See Is What You Get." WYSIWYG showed words on the screen exactly as they would appear on paper, whether printed in italics, boldface, or another typestyle.

Although Bill had decided to focus on software, he made a few exceptions. He ordered the creation of a piece of hardware, a mouse that would be used with an upcoming GUI program. He formed Microsoft Press, which published books about how to use Microsoft programs. He opened offices and licensed other companies to sell Microsoft products in Japan, Europe, and Australia.

Microsoft continued its relationship with IBM, licensing MS-DOS for IBM's new, powerful IBM PC-AT. In a joint venture, programmers at the two companies began to develop a more advanced operating system, OS/2. But each development team had a different idea of what the end product should include and how it should work. Eventually IBM went on to finish OS/2 by itself, leaving out many facets that Microsoft had brought to the project.

Working on Windows

Instead of OS/2, Bill Gates bet the future of his company on an operating system he called Windows. Windows, named for the separate frames users could create on the computer screen, would feature the graphical user interface (the mouse). Instead of memorizing commands, users would operate the computer with a mouse, pointing and clicking on small pictures called icons. Windows would be user friendly. It would let people run more than one program at a time—a process called multitasking—and it would let them easily move information from one program to another.

Bill had big plans for Windows. He spent hours considering what the program would look like and how it would work. Should the windows overlap or appear next to one another? What should the icons look like? What colors should the borders, titles, and all the other visual elements on the screen be?

The thirty programmers who worked on the first version of Windows thrived on the challenge of creating an exciting new

Leading the way: Bill worked hard to create the Windows program and expected his employees to work hard as well.

product. They often worked extremely long hours, sometimes to the point of exhaustion, to meet deadlines.

By 1984 Windows was way behind schedule. Bill often asked programmers to make changes in the program, sometimes requiring them to throw out weeks' worth of computer code and start over. This atmosphere could be frustrating for programmers and stressful for managers, several of whom left the company, "unable to tolerate the screaming fits [Bill] and Ballmer threw." According to Ballmer, Bill even threatened to fire him over the delays, although Bill later called the threat a joke.

Like the programmers, Bill maintained a hectic work schedule. Along with Steve Ballmer, he was the head salesperson for Microsoft products. And he liked to know what was going on in all areas of Microsoft—and have his say about it.

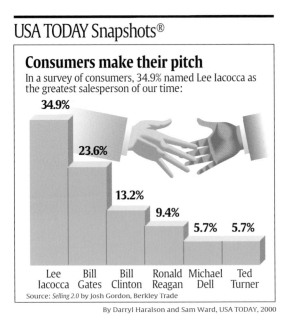

USA TODAY Snapshots®

Consumers make their pitch

In a survey of consumers, 34.9% named Lee Iacocca as the greatest salesperson of our time:

34.9%	23.6%	13.2%	9.4%	5.7%	5.7%
Lee Iacocca	Bill Gates	Bill Clinton	Ronald Reagan	Michael Dell	Ted Turner

Source: *Selling 2.0* by Josh Gordon, Berkley Trade

By Darryl Haralson and Sam Ward, USA TODAY, 2000

Social Life

Bill didn't have much time for life outside of work. In 1983 he bought a house in his parents' neighborhood. The house had an indoor swimming pool but little furniture. The den contained a desk cluttered with computer magazines and a computer. An e-mail system allowed Microsoft employees to send messages to one another's computers at work. Since Bill's home computer was tied into the system via phone lines, he could send messages to his employees from home. And he did—sometimes in the middle of the night.

Despite all the work, Bill made a point to see his family on a regular basis. He sometimes had friends over for parties or to swim in his indoor pool. For a long time, Bill had no television—he was afraid it would distract him from his work. Finally, a friend gave him a television that was adjusted to play only videos.

As male coworkers got married, Bill threw bachelor parties. He himself had several girlfriends. For a year, he dated Jill Bennett, a sales representative from another computer company. Bill and Jill shared an interest in computers and tennis and had some friends in common. What they didn't have enough of, though, was time. Bill boasted of his seven-hour turnaround time, meaning he was back at the office only seven hours after leaving for the day. He felt dating took too much time and energy.

Another girlfriend was software entrepreneur and investor Ann Winblad, whom Bill met at a computer conference in 1984. They dated on and off for three years. They studied physics together and went on educational vacations to places like South America and Africa. While visiting the rain forests of Brazil,

Close friend: Ann Winblad, also a software engineer, dated Bill for three years beginning in 1984.

they studied biotechnology. In Africa they learned about evolution from a famous anthropologist. "To Bill, life is school," Ann explained. "There's always something more to learn." Ann, several years older than Bill, was ready to settle down. But Bill wasn't ready for marriage. After he and Ann stopped dating, they remained friends.

 A slender and healthy person, Ann Winblad persuaded fast-food junkie Bill to give up his favorite food—cheeseburgers—for a time.

Computer success: Microsoft was selling millions of dollars' worth of products by 1984. Software for computers, like the one shown above, was the company's focus.

Ten Years in the Making

In 1985 Bill celebrated his thirtieth birthday with a roller-skating party for family, friends, and coworkers. This year also marked the tenth anniversary of Microsoft. For a decade, Bill had focused intensely on his business. His dedication was paying off. In 1985 the company sold $140 million in products, including operating systems, business software, hardware, and how-to books.

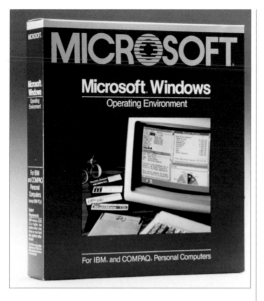

Beginning of the Windows era: Microsoft Windows in its original packaging

Even better, the first version of Windows had been sold in the United States that year. Windows had a few bugs, and other computer companies hadn't yet written many programs to run with it. Some computer industry specialists wondered if Windows' GUI system was really the future of personal computing. But for Bill Gates, Windows was only the beginning.

He had never imagined that his company would grow so big so fast. In fact, he had wanted to keep the staff at about one thousand employees. Yet Microsoft continued to grow, with MS-DOS bringing in steady income. The company grew so fast that Bill no longer knew the names of all his employees.

As such a powerful company, Microsoft has been accused of "borrowing" ideas for programs from smaller companies in ways that are, while not necessarily illegal, at least perceived as unfair. According to such accusations, Microsoft and a company would discuss a partnership, in which the small firm would benefit from Microsoft's size and influence, while Microsoft would benefit from collaborating on a project already in development. Several of these companies, such as Micrografx and Go, have claimed that Microsoft looked at their ideas and then chose to end the partnership, later releasing similar, competing products. Bill has denied all charges of "pilfering," or stealing, saying that Microsoft simply builds upon the technology that already exists. No legal action was taken at the time.

In 1986 Microsoft moved its corporate headquarters to the outskirts of Redmond, Washington, constructing four X-shaped buildings in an industrial park. In the middle of these buildings was an artificial lake that soon became known as Lake Bill. Every employee had an office with a computer, a high-quality chair, and a nice woodsy view. Nearby canteens offered free beverages. Candy and other snacks were available at a low cost. If the weather cooperated, workers grabbed food from the cafeteria and headed for spots on the lawn. There, people played musical instruments, juggled, rode unicycles, and played basketball, soccer, and softball.

Microsoft's home: This aerial view shows the sprawling Microsoft campus.

As the company roster expanded from one thousand to more than twenty thousand employees, Microsoft constructed more buildings. Its facilities eventually took up the whole office park. Yet one thing remained basically the same—the flat corporate structure. "Flat" meant that there were just enough managers to keep the programmers, marketing staff, and customer service specialists moving along at their jobs. With e-mail, employees could quickly send memos to many people at once, so the company needed few secretaries. Staff could and did e-mail Bill directly with their ideas, questions, and gripes.

USA TODAY Snapshots®

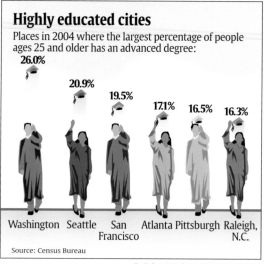

Highly educated cities

Places in 2004 where the largest percentage of people ages 25 and older has an advanced degree:

26.0% Washington
20.9% Seattle
19.5% San Francisco
17.1% Atlanta
16.5% Pittsburgh
16.3% Raleigh, N.C.

Source: Census Bureau

By Robert W. Ahrens, USA TODAY, 2005

Going Public

During Microsoft's first decade, Bill gave many employees stock options—shares of the company that represented part ownership. As long as Microsoft was privately owned, employees could not sell their shares. In 1986 Microsoft "went public," selling shares on the stock exchange to institutions and people who were not employees. As a publicly owned company, Microsoft could sell stock at whatever price people were willing to pay.

Some businesses sell shares of stock to generate money for expansion. But Microsoft did not need to generate money. It had no debt and had made a profit of $30 million during the first six months of 1985. Yet Bill did need to keep his hardworking employees happy. The morning that Microsoft stock first went on sale, it sold at $21 per share. By the end of that day, the price had risen to $28 per share. Microsoft employees who had been given stock options year after year could trade their stock for cash or keep it in case the price went higher, which it did.

Money

SECTION B

November 29, 1996

Microsoft Research: R&D without Ivory Tower

From the Pages of USA TODAY

Bill Gates is bursting to talk about the $2 billion a year Microsoft spends on research and development. The Microsoft CEO has been bringing it up everywhere: in his keynote speech at last week's Comdex computer show; in conversations with reporters and analysts; in talks with customers.

Walk the halls of Building 9 on Microsoft's vast campus and you can see much of what Gates gets for his $2 billion.

There's Jim Kajiya—long hair, sideburns, shirt pocket stuffed with a fistful of papers and pens—showing technology that eventually can help ordinary users of ordinary personal computers create 3-D graphics that rival those of *Toy Story*. In another door is X.D. Huang, who is teaching PCs to listen and talk, a project that could save all of Asia from becoming a technology backwater. Remember, Huang says, that the Chinese language has 60,000 characters, which pretty much keeps 2 billion people from using a keyboard when interacting with a computer.

Bell Labs and IBM's Watson Research lab feel scientific—with big open rooms jammed with futuristic-looking gadgets

Whiteboards: New facilities at Microsoft, like this one built in 2006, still feature areas where workers can gather to brainstorm and write ideas on a whiteboard.

and scruffy offices hit by blizzards of paper. Microsoft Research veers more toward a hushed insurance company headquarters. A maze of carpeted hallways leads past modest-size offices, most amazingly tidy. The research happens at desktop computers or in meetings that typically feature lots of scribbling on a whiteboard.

—Kevin Maney, November 29, 1996

As the stock became more valuable, some people, including Bill Gates and Steve Ballmer, became instant millionaires—at least on paper. If they wanted cash, they'd have to sell their shares of stock. Bill sold over $1 million worth of stock, but he still owned more Microsoft stock than any other employee—45 percent of all the shares.

IN F⊕CUS

Multi-Multimillionaires

Bill worried that Microsoft employees might become distracted by watching the company's stock price on the stock market. He didn't want employees daydreaming about elaborate houses, fancy cars, or other luxuries that they might buy as their stock rose in value. He also feared that some of his best employees might retire after becoming millionaires. Yet, to his pleasant surprise, most employees—even the hundreds of newly made millionaires—continued to come to work every day.

Millionaire club: Bill *(front)* with Steve Ballmer *(left)* and other executives at the Microsoft campus

Becoming a millionaire did not change Bill much. He agonized over buying a speedboat. Although he did take a four-day sailing trip in Australia to celebrate the success of the stock offering, he returned to work with the same drive as always. He traveled cheaply on business trips. He drove his own car instead of hiring a limousine. He carried his own baggage at airports. And he still ordered his favorite cheeseburgers at fast-food restaurants.

Microgames

Bill's grandmother died in 1987. In her honor, Bill bought 3.5 acres (1.4 hectares) on the Hood Canal and built a retreat, dubbed Cheerio, for family gatherings. The property included three vacation homes, tennis courts, and a spa. He also built a large structure that could be used as a business retreat. "The idea was really a tribute to [Gam], being that she was the glue that kept our family together. And that we wanted to preserve that very special opportunity for us to find times to be together even though everyone's life was moving off in different directions," Mary Gates explained.

The retreat became the site of the Microgames, a festival for friends, family, and Microsoft employees, started in 1986. At the Microgames, the Gates clan acted as organizers and judges. The guests were to have all the fun. Divided into teams, they solved puzzles, sang, raced, and went on treasure hunts. Each year the games had a different theme. One year guests found themselves on an African safari, another year in the Wild West.

At the 1987 Microgames, Bill met Melinda French, a new Microsoft employee. Bill was immediately attracted to the smart, witty, and independent Melinda. She had grown up in Dallas, Texas, with two brothers and a sister. Like her father, an aerospace engineer, Melinda found math exciting. She had studied computer science and economics at Duke University in Durham, North Carolina, earning her undergraduate degree in only three years. She then earned a master's degree from Duke's business school, where a Microsoft recruiting team recognized

New friend: Melinda French had a lot in common with Bill when they met in 1987.

her talent. After a round of interviews at the Redmond offices, French joined Microsoft. Upon meeting at the Microgames, she and Bill began dating.

Riding the Wave

Microsoft continued to bring new products to the marketplace. In 1987 it introduced its second version of Windows and its Excel spreadsheet software. The following year, the company's manufacturing and distribution center moved to a larger facility in Bothell, Washington. A new product support center answered more than one million customer calls each month.

On the same day in 1986 that Microsoft had moved into its headquarters in Redmond, it held its first conference on CD-ROMs (compact discs with read-only memory). CD-ROMs looked like the next hot product. They were multimedia CDs that could hold far more data than existing computer diskettes. In 1987 Microsoft sold its first CD-ROM, Microsoft Bookshelf, a single CD that held ten popular and useful reference books. When computer manufacturers made CD-ROM readers common on their new computers, Microsoft was ready.

With his company firmly established in Redmond, Bill decided it was time to think about building a house for himself. In 1988 and 1989, he bought parcels of land in Medina, a city on the shores of Lake Washington, 2 miles (3.2 km) across the lake from his parents' home.

Bill continued to think ahead. Knowing that graphic designers and publishers would soon be working with digital images—pictures that are scanned and stored by computers—he founded a company called Corbis. Corbis bought millions of works of art and photography, including the famous Bettmann Archive of photographs.

Corbis owns one of the largest collections of images in the world, with more than 100 million current and historic photographs. The company serves businesses and people in more than fifty countries.

The Corbis collection is stored in an online database. It holds pictures in many subject areas: fine arts, history, people, cultures, entertainment, science, technology, and nature. For a fee, publishers can use these images in books, magazines, newspapers, or online publications. Corbis can also print posters for buyers or take them on computerized trips around the world.

Photo collector: Bill looks through the photo archives of his new company, Corbis.

Windows wizard: Bill shows off the latest version of Windows in 1990. Microsoft kicked off the launch of Windows 3.0 with a presentation in New York City.

Finding Balance

On May 22, 1990, Bill Gates pushed his glasses up his nose, grinned, and walked onstage at Center City in New York City. He was there to launch Windows 3.0—the third version of Windows. In the audience and via television, thousands of reporters and computer employees watched the presentation. Industry leaders praised the new Windows. A short, MTV-style video hyped the program and kicked off a six-month advertising campaign. Microsoft had spent $3 million on the launch day alone and more than $10 million total to make Windows 3.0 the fastest-moving software product in the country.

In the first two weeks after its release, buyers snapped up more than one hundred thousand copies of Windows 3.0. By the end of 1991, Microsoft had shipped four million copies in twelve languages to twenty-four countries. As part of the Windows Ready-to-Run program, some computer manufacturers were including Windows as standard software on their computers. Even the Microsoft mouse was swept up in the surge—buyers trapped six million. Bill finally had a software best-seller.

Other Interests

During this time, he continued to think about his dream house. To find a plan he liked, he hired an architect to run an international design competition. The winner was a house to be made of concrete, steel, wood, and stone. It would not overpower the site. It would nestle into a hillside, with lots of windows to offer lake and mountain views. "I wanted craftsmanship but nothing ostentatious," explained Bill.

Also on Bill's mind were investments outside of Microsoft. As a child, he had dreamed about becoming a scientist. He had long been interested in biotechnology, evolution, the brain, and DNA. "I'm sometimes asked what field I would have chosen if not computers," Bill said. "It's hard to say for sure, but I've always been fascinated by biology and genetics."

Biotechnology involves using technology to make biological discoveries and products. In 1990 three scientists who had already made important medical discoveries invited Bill to invest in their new biotechnology company, ICOS, and to join its board of directors. Bill studied the scientists' prospectus and invested $5 million.

ICOS was the first of several biotech companies Bill backed. Why would someone as rich as Bill Gates invest in new businesses? He didn't need to make more money. Instead, Bill wanted to use his money to advance technology and help people.

In October 1991, Bill gave $12 million to create a department of molecular biology at the University of Washington. With this new department, the university was able to convince a famous geneticist, Leroy Hood, to do research there. Hood is a leader in mapping genes in the human body. His work might lead to cures for fatal diseases. Before making his donation, Bill had studied Hood's research on DNA and had met with him.

A few months earlier, in July 1991, Mary Gates had called her son and said that she wanted him to meet another famous person—billionaire investor Warren Buffett. Though Bill said he was very busy, he and Melinda flew by helicopter to Cheerio, the family summer home,

IN FOCUS

Warren Buffett

Born in Nebraska in 1930, Warren Buffett began making business decisions at an early age. At the age of eleven, he'd bought his first stock— and was patient enough to wait for it to make money. He started a small investment company in the late 1950s. And by the late 1960s, he had a large and varied set of investments that was making him a rich man.

By the early 1990s, when Buffett met Bill Gates, Buffett was a billionaire and one of the world's wealthiest people. He's remained a down-to-earth person, though, and still lives in the house he bought early in his career.

Stock market mogul: Warren Buffett in 1989

where Buffett and other guests had gathered. Immediately, Gates and Buffett hit it off. They found they had much in common, including a keen mind for business, a sense of humor, and a fondness for hamburgers. At Buffett's suggestion, Bill again took up playing bridge. At Bill's suggestion, the non-computer-savvy Buffett joined an online bridge club and became a computer user. Buffett called Bill's business sense extraordinary. "If Bill had started a hot dog stand, he would have become the hot dog king of the world," Buffett declared.

Personal and Professional Progress

Though Windows 3.0 was a best-seller, Bill didn't rest. By 1992 programmers had improved Windows in a thousand ways. Bill knew that if he didn't keep improving a product greatly, no one would want to buy new versions—they would just keep using the old one. Microsoft continued to improve not only Windows but also Microsoft's other programs. For example, the company offered its Word 2.0 word-processing program in twenty-two different languages.

While Bill worked to improve Microsoft products, builders began excavating the site for his dream home. Because Seattle is located in an earthquake zone, the design required tons of concrete and many beams and supports. For beams, builders recycled Douglas fir timbers from a lumber mill that was being torn down.

Never satisfied: Bill was busy in the mid-1990s working on improvements to Windows and other Microsoft products and overseeing work on his new home.

USA TODAY

News

SECTION A

September 30, 1996

No place like home for Gates— a $40M home

<u>From the Pages of USA TODAY</u>

Lavish multimillion-dollar homes are common in this affluent enclave that is home to old Seattle money and new high-tech millionaires.

But few here have seen anything quite like the digs Microsoft Chairman Bill Gates is building in this quiet community of 3,000 set amid winding, wooded lanes.

Six years in the making, Gates' residential vision has taken three times longer to build than nearby Seattle's tallest building—the 76-story Columbia Seafirst Center.

As construction finally winds down, the cost of his waterfront estate is approaching $40 million. With 35,000 square feet of living space it is more than 20 times larger than most American homes.

Gates, 40, is building on five lots of prime property along Lake Washington. Projected completion is late this year—at least a year overdue.

One reason for the delay, local newspapers reported, was Gates' 1994 marriage to Microsoft executive Melinda French. She reportedly scanned the original plans and said, "I'm not living in that!"

So they huddled with architects and designers and came up with some new plans. The project has lasted, Gates says, "for what seems like most of my life."

He hopes to move in sometime next year with his wife and infant, Jennifer Katharine. For now the Gateses live about a half-mile away in a comparatively modest 4,000-square-foot waterfront house.

Construction of the Gates "convention center," as some call the project, has riled some neighbors, though many say Gates has gone out of his way to smooth over bad feelings.

"I think they've done a marvelous job," says retired builder Maurice Mylroie, a Medina resident for 60 years.

The workers wave to neighbors and don't begin work until 7:30 a.m. They could start as early as 7:00 a.m.

"The crew is nice and they can't do enough for you," says a woman whose china cabinet was shaken by construction activity. Gates' workers helped pack her china securely.

All is not goodness and light. Ex-city councilwoman Sigrid Guyton and her husband, Steven, complained bitterly about dust and noise coming from the construction site. The Guytons, who are physicians, say the dust caused breathing problems for them and their two children. They got so frustrated that they moved to Seattle this year and no longer will speak about the matter.

Meanwhile, the estate has become one of the attractions on cruises of Lake Washington. "It looks like a hotel," says Kathleen Bailey, 33, of Loves Park, Ill.

British software engineer Michael Peters, 31, thinks the home "is a bit extreme. . . . but he has some nice views."

Gates, whose fortune is put at $18 billion by Forbes magazine's ranking of the world's richest people, hired Pacific Northwest architect James Cutler, who designs houses to fit natural landscapes.

Cutler seldom uses a computer, considers television antisocial, and works in a converted boathouse on Bainbridge Island, near Seattle. Most of his houses are less than 5,000 square feet.

Cutler and project partner Peter Bohlin of Wilkes-Barre, Pa., want the grounds to revert back to forest, not lawn.

The Gates home in Medina, Washington

Much of the house will be underground, with seven wood and stone pavilions visible from the water. Skylights and windows will admit as much sunshine as the oft-gloomy Northwest skies offer.

Neighbor Robert Romano says the Gates home blends in with its surroundings. "If you walk down there it's like going into an ancient forest," he said.

"On the outside, you do have a house that has none of the palatial qualities of Donald Trump's estate, but on the inside, the glitz comes out," says Mark Alan Hewitt, an architect and historian who has written about tycoons and their mansions. "High tech becomes the thing that is consumed with virtually unlimited display."

In architectural circles, the buzz is over how Cutler and New York society architect Thierry Despont are meshing. Despont was hired for interior design after the marriage. None of the team will talk. Contractors and suppliers signed confidentiality agreements.

—Dee Ann Glamser, September 30, 1996

Inside the house, a master computer would run the lights, temperature controls, security system, and other features. Flat LCDs (liquid-crystal displays) on the walls would be programmed to show different pieces of artwork. Explained Bill, "I wanted a house that would accommodate sophisticated, changing technology, but in an unobtrusive way that made it clear that technology was the servant, not the master."

The rooms in Bill's home are programmed to play the occupants' favorite music when they enter the room.

The builders worked first on the guesthouse, so they could use it to test another new technology. High-bandwidth wiring would allow the computers running the house to be superfast.

Settling Down

With her combination of intelligence and people skills, Melinda French rose quickly through the ranks at Microsoft. By 1993 she was the product unit manager for Microsoft Publisher, a desktop publishing system. She supervised the work of about forty employees.

Since meeting at the Microgames in 1987, Bill and Melinda had dated on and off. On business trips, Bill sometimes went out with other women, but when he was in town, he gravitated toward Melinda. The couple went to dinner, movies, and plays. Once they took a trip to Australia. It became obvious to people who knew Bill well that he and Melinda had something special.

Bill's parents were concerned about him. He seemed to be too busy with work to have time for love. So after Bill and Melinda had been dating for some time, Bill's mother asked him when he was going to give Melinda an engagement ring. Finally, on March 20, 1993, Bill surprised Melinda. On a chartered flight from Palm Springs, California, to Seattle, Bill arranged for a detour to Omaha, Nebraska.

Together time: Bill and Melinda live a high-profile life. Here, they are going to a Planet Hollywood restaurant opening.

There, Warren Buffett met the couple. Buffett had arranged for a famous jewelry store to be opened for them alone. The couple picked out a diamond engagement ring.

Two days later, the public relations department at Microsoft announced the engagement. The news made headlines around the world. Many people who knew Bill and Melinda thought they were well matched. "She's really a wonderful person, the perfect match for him," said Bill Gates Sr. "Very, very bright, very organized, very supportive, very interested in family and good family life."

Melinda could give Bill personal happiness and could understand his business, which was such an important part of his life. Yet she was concerned that by marrying the richest man in the world, she would lose her privacy. She did not want to be fodder for the newspapers. So she contacted relatives, friends, and former neighbors and teachers. She asked them not to talk about her to reporters. She was also concerned for her safety—being so wealthy could make her a target for kidnappers.

 Since Melinda and Bill were going to live together after their wedding, Melinda wanted some changes made to the house under construction. She didn't care for the exposed beams and rough concrete. She wanted her own study and a dressing room. She wanted a kitchen that would suit a family instead of just a noncooking bachelor. And she wanted security people for protection and privacy.

On the business front, Bill was taking Microsoft full speed into multimedia products. In 1993 Microsoft began to sell more CD-ROM titles. These included Microsoft Encarta, the first multimedia encyclopedia designed for a computer. With sound, animation, illustrations, graphs, maps, and photographs, Encarta brought subjects to life. Later, Microsoft sold other CDs, some of which focused on specific subjects such as dinosaurs, movies, music, baseball, and golf.

Too Close for Comfort

Melinda knew that her marriage to Bill would force her to leave her job at Microsoft. Even before the marriage actually took place, the people Melinda had been working with became uncomfortable with her personal connection to the company's owner. Perhaps they feared that their complaints about the company might get back to their boss. Instead of working at Microsoft, Melinda would sit on boards of directors of other companies and work for charitable organizations.

Melinda French Gates

For the business world, Microsoft brought out its high-powered Windows NT (New Technology) operating system. With this software, businesspeople could run a whole network of computer terminals from a single PC. They could keep track of how many products they had in storage. They could keep track of sales and how much money their company earned. They could do complicated calculations. *PC Magazine* gave Windows NT an award for technical excellence.

USA TODAY

CHAPTER FIVE

Private ceremony: Although no reporters were allowed on the Hawaiian island during Bill and Melinda's wedding ceremony, some managed to take photographs from boats. Bill and Melinda are to the left, facing the edge of the cliff.

Life in the Spotlight

Bill and Melinda made arrangements to marry on January 1, 1994, on the island of Lanai in Hawaii. They chose the island because it is privately owned and they could control who would attend the wedding. No party crashers were allowed, especially uninvited photographers. Just 130 invited guests would be there.

Bill paid for the guests, many of them rich and famous themselves, to stay at a hotel on the island. The day before the wedding, the male guests played golf and ate lunch with the groom. The female guests attended a luncheon for the bride. That night Bill and Melinda treated guests to a luau (a Hawaiian outdoor party). As a surprise for his wife-to-be, Bill arranged for her favorite singer, Willie Nelson, to perform. Melinda was delighted. Everyone danced on the beach. The evening ended with a dazzling fireworks show.

Though Bill and Melinda tried to keep the date and place of their wedding a secret, word leaked out. The story made the newspapers. But security people turned away reporters who tried to get to the island.

On their wedding day, Melinda wore a white silk-faced organza wedding gown strewn with pearls. Five bridesmaids in pink gowns attended her. Bill wore a white dinner jacket and black trousers. Steve Ballmer was his best man.

On a cliff high above the Pacific Ocean, at the twelfth tee of a golf course, Bill and Melinda exchanged vows. Melinda, a devout Catholic, wanted a religious wedding. At the end of the short Roman Catholic ceremony, Bill slipped a wedding ring on Melinda's finger. They kissed as the setting

Wedding celebration: Bill and Melinda had a party in Seattle with friends and family to celebrate their marriage the week after the ceremony.

sun cast a pink glow over the sky. "We're both extremely happy and looking forward to a long, wonderful life together," Bill later announced to the public.

Yet in life, joy and sorrow often intermingle, and for Bill Gates, fate did not make an exception. Shortly before he and Melinda married, Bill learned that his mother was battling breast cancer. Though she had the best care possible, the cancer overtook her within a year. In the early morning of June 10, 1994, Mary Gates died.

Bill and his mother had been very close, and her death hit him hard. When he heard the news, he got in his car and rushed to his parents' house. On the way, a police officer pulled him over for speeding. The officer recognized Bill and, seeing tears streaming down his face, asked what had happened. A choked-up Bill explained that his mother had just died. The officer waved Bill on, gently admonishing him to drive a little slower.

Several days later, Bill spoke at his mother's memorial service, which was packed with family, friends, and colleagues. Then he turned to his family and work for solace. Melinda helped see him through the difficult months that followed.

Money to Burn

The Federal Trade Commission (FTC) is a government agency that keeps watch over large and successful companies to make sure they conduct their business legally. In 1991 the FTC and the U.S. Department of Justice began to investigate Microsoft. In 1994 Justice Department lawyers sued Microsoft over its sales practices.

Microsoft had always insisted that computer makers who sold the Microsoft operating system had to sell other Microsoft products as well. The lawsuit put an end to this practice, which was considered illegal. Even so, Bill Gates did not admit that his company had done anything wrong.

As the value of Microsoft stock continued to rise, Bill became a billionaire, passing Warren Buffett to top the list of Amreica's richest people.

October 3, 1994

'Forbes' list starts at $310M: Richest from high tech companies

<u>From the Pages of</u>
<u>USA TODAY</u>

How much does it take to be considered really rich these days?

To qualify for *Forbes* magazine's 1994 list of the richest 400 people in America, you had to have $310 million, more than twice what it took 12 years ago, accounting for inflation.

In the past 10 years, the biggest fortunes have been built in high technology, communications, retailing, entertainment and high finance. In fact, nearly 40 percent of the 400 richest people now come from those industries vs. 20 percent a decade ago. Back then, the richest clumped in the real estate, oil and gas industries.

But inflation ebbed, making "hard assets less valuable (and) ideas and innovation more valuable," the magazine states. Consider the richest of all. Bill Gates, founder and CEO of Microsoft, built his fortune by creating computer programs. In addition to a 25 percent stake in Microsoft, he has also invested in communications and bio-technology.

Other high-techies ranking high: Oracle CEO Lawrence Ellison and former Microsoft executive Paul Allen, now an investor.

Investing wizard Warren Buffett led the financial players, including Edward Crosby Johnson 3d and family, which runs mutual fund giant Fidelity Investment. Johnson surged to fourth on the list from 38th last year, as the investment firm flourished.

Other investor-finance types that ranked high: Ronald Perelman, Kirk Kerkorian, George Soros and Tisch brothers Laurence and Preston.

Entertainment and media magnates fared well, paced by John Kluge, CEO of Metromedia; publishing titans Sam and Don Newhouse, and Viacom Chairman Sumner Redstone.

Leading the retailers: Amway founders Richard Marvin DeVos and Jay Van Andel, who surged into the top 10 as their people-to-people sales company thrived. Members of Walmart founder Sam Walton's family also ranked high.

—James Kim, October 3, 1994

With $525,000 a year in salary and bonuses, Bill was actually not the highest-paid employee at Microsoft. But he sold shares in the company at regular intervals, using money from the sales to pay his taxes, build his home, and invest in other businesses.

Bill didn't show off his wealth. He tried to keep a low profile. To reporters, Bill Gates was a commodity. He was a celebrity, and he couldn't avoid the media. But Bill thought

Speaking his mind: Bill speaks at a computer trade show in Las Vegas, Nevada, in 1994.

that talking to reporters was a waste of time. He was impatient with what he called "stupid questions," and he earned a reputation for rudeness. When one television reporter stated that competing with Microsoft was like being in a knife fight, Bill lost his temper and walked off the stage.

One Bill watcher figured out that he earned about $150 each second. At that pay rate, it wouldn't be worthwhile for Bill to pick a $500 bill off the sidewalk. He could earn more money just by walking on.

Some critics focused on Bill's wealth. When he donated millions of dollars to charity, people openly questioned his motives or criticized the amount or timing of the donation. For example, when the Gates Library Foundation began donating computers to libraries, some detractors suggested that Bill just wanted to sell more software to the libraries. Other critics simply said that he hadn't donated enough.

Expanding opportunities: Bill looks on as children use computers during an event hosted by the Gates Library Foundation.

Giving Back

Calling himself a "steward of a share of society's resources," in 1994 Bill announced plans to return his money to society in positive ways. "Giving away money effectively is almost as hard as earning it in the first place," he once said. That year he and Melinda created the William H. Gates Foundation, which would funnel money to

Father's role: William H. Gates Sr., shown here in 1997, ran Bill's charity foundation when it was formed.

worthy projects. Bill's father, William H. Gates Sr., retired from his law firm to run the foundation.

The foundation focused on four areas: education, worldwide public health and population issues, nonprofit civic and arts organizations, and campaigns to create endowments (such as scholarships) in the Puget Sound area. Bill and Melinda also donated $1 million to the Fred Hutchinson Cancer Research Center in Seattle.

In recalling his school years, Bill said: "Letting students use a computer in the late 1960s was a pretty amazing choice at the time in Seattle—and one I'll always be grateful for." Paul Allen, recovered from his illness, had stayed with Microsoft as a member of its board of directors. Bill and Paul showed their gratitude by paying for a new science building at Lakeside School. The two friends flipped a coin to decide whose name would go first on the building. Inside Allen-Gates Hall, they named the auditorium in memory of their classmate Kent Evans. Along with Steve Ballmer, Bill also paid for a new computer center for Harvard University. The price tag: $15 million from Bill, and $10 million from Ballmer.

IN FOCUS

Codex Leicester

Some of Bill's investments were made for personal reasons. In 1994 the Codex Leicester, a scientific notebook written by Leonardo da Vinci, was put up for sale. In the eighteen-page notebook, Leonardo wrote about many subjects: astronomy, geology, paleontology, and hydraulics. A fan of Leonardo since boyhood, Bill paid $30.8 million for the unique masterpiece. "Leonardo was one of the most amazing people who ever lived. He was a genius in more fields than any scientist of any age and an astonishing painter and sculptor," Bill explained with enthusiasm. "I bought the manuscript for personal pleasure." When not on loan to museums, the Codex Leicester would be housed in Bill's personal library.

Historic document: This is a manuscript page from the Codex Leicester. Bill bought Leonardo da Vinci's scientific notebook in 1994 for $30.8 million.

Exploring the Future

Bill Gates has said that the growth of the Internet—the worldwide network of connected computers—is the most important event since the creation of the personal computer. The Internet started as a network of government computers in the 1970s. At first only scientists and military officials used the Internet. When businesspeople discovered the system, they wanted to use it to advertise products and services. Schools and libraries realized that the system could be used to spread information. As more organizations began posting material on the Internet, the World Wide Web was born.

As early as 1994, Microsoft added hypertext markup language (HTML) to its word-processing system. HTML is used to create Web pages. But creating tools for the Internet wasn't Bill Gates's top goal in 1994. "Getting Windows 95 done was the top priority; getting Windows NT to critical mass in the market was the top priority," Bill remembered.

Changing times: In 1994 Bill was still focused on getting Windows 95 done and had not yet realized how the Internet would change the computer industry.

IN FOCUS

Teledesic

In 1994 Bill joined Craig McCaw, a pioneer in the world of cellular telephones, in an ambitious venture. They created a company called Teledesic. Its goal was to circle Earth with 288 low-orbiting satellites that would provide two-way communications for the entire world. Each of the satellites would cost nearly $20 million to build, so Teledesic needed many investors.

"I am investing in Teledesic because I believe it is a very exciting idea with the potential to truly connect the world together in a way it never has been before," Bill said. The network would give people in areas without basic telephone service the ability to communicate using hand-held devices. The project proved to be too ambitious, though, and Teledesic closed its doors for good in 2002.

Late in 1994, however, Bill realized what some of his employees had already been trying to tell him—that the Internet would be the communication tool of the future. He realized that he had better make quick changes at Microsoft. Otherwise, his company would be left in the dust of other companies that were making software for the Internet.

On May 26, 1995, Bill wrote a long e-mail memo to his employees. In "The Internet Tidal Wave," he announced, "Now I assign the Internet the highest level of importance. In this memo I want to make clear that our focus on the Internet is critical to every part of our business." Bill was energized.

He asked leaders of all the project groups in Microsoft to add Internet communication and information retrieval features to their programs. They started by adding a Web browser, Internet Explorer, to the newest Windows operating system. The browser let PC users bring Internet sites to their own computer screens. Later in 1995, Bill

Focusing on the web: The monitor in the background shows a version of Microsoft's Web browser, Internet Explorer.

announced his plan to supply software for networks of computers that could work together over the Internet. Microsoft would also develop software for creating websites with graphics, animation, video, and audio. It would make software for companies that put websites on the Internet. Bill described the new focus: "We are as focused on the Internet as we were on graphical computing—all of our products treat the Internet as the big opportunity."

Meanwhile, in a personal effort, Bill and Melinda made a special gift to honor Bill's mother, Mary. On the anniversary of her death, they donated $10 million to the University of Washington to establish the Mary Gates Endowment for Students. Mary had always placed a high value on education. With this scholarship, many undergraduate students would benefit.

Windows 95

In mid-1995, Microsoft launched Windows 95. It was a new operating system—and a whole lot more. The system included CD, fax, and modem software. More important, its overall design was simple and clean. It made complicated jobs easy to perform.

On August 24, fifteen large white tents decorated the lawn outside Microsoft headquarters in Redmond. A circuslike atmosphere prevailed. The first tent featured Bill Gates and special guest Jay Leno, host of *The Tonight Show*. The fourteen other tents held representatives from software companies demonstrating programs designed to run on Windows 95.

Bill came onstage wearing white slacks and a navy blue sport shirt bearing the Windows logo. He and Leno traded jokes. Saying that Bill wasn't so smart, Leno added that he'd once gone to Bill's home and found the VCR flashing twelve o'clock. Gesturing at Leno, Bill quipped, "Windows 95 is so easy, even a talk show host can figure it out." Then Leno introduced Windows 95 to twenty-five hundred specially invited people—five

Windows launch: Jay Leno *(right)*, host of *The Tonight Show with Jay Leno*, was invited to be a special guest at the kickoff event for Windows 95 software.

Talking up Windows: Bill relaxes between interviews while promoting Windows 95.

hundred of them journalists from more than thirty countries. They had all come to get a look at the fruit of two years of work writing 15 million lines of computer code.

As Windows 95 was coming out, Microsoft also launched its own online service, Microsoft Network (MSN). As with other online services, people could pay Microsoft a fee each month for Internet connection. Then they could use Internet features such as e-mail, news services, banking services, and chat rooms. Though Windows 95 sold rapidly, not many users joined the new online network. But if at first it didn't succeed, Microsoft would try again. Within a year, it had redesigned MSN. People began to join the network, but not in big enough numbers to give Microsoft a profit.

Home and Abroad

With the launch of Windows 95 behind him, Bill took time off to travel. With a group of friends, including Bill Gates Sr. and Warren Buffett,

Bill and Melinda took a two-week trip to China. They traveled by train and boat through the country. At the Great Wall of China, Bill tried to fly a kite, but the wind wouldn't cooperate. When not viewing the scenery or sightseeing, Bill played bridge. Melinda also organized fun activities, like karaoke singing and trivia quizzes.

> While in China, Bill bought a 9-foot-tall (3 meters) clay statue of a Chinese warrior as a souvenir. It was a replica of a famous statue that had been unearthed by archaeologists.

In the capital city of Beijing, Bill met with Chinese leader and Communist Party president Jiang Zemin. Bill, Melinda, and Warren Buffett posed for photos with Jiang. Ever the businessman, Bill paid a quick visit to Microsoft's Beijing office.

Seeing only golf: Bill is an avid golfer. He celebrated his birthday in 1995 with a party featuring miniature golf.

Bill celebrated his fortieth birthday with a party at his new but still unfinished home. Bill had taken up golf. So for this special occasion, Melinda arranged for an eighteen-hole miniature golf course to be set up on the grounds. She and Bill dressed in old-fashioned golfing clothes, and the eighty guests came in costume too. As a birthday surprise, Melinda invited four of his female friends to come dressed as cheerleaders. Their lettered sweaters spelled out *B-I-L-L.*

Bill decided that it would be worthwhile to educate the public about computers and Microsoft. He began writing a newspaper column, published by the *New York Times* syndicate and on Microsoft's website. In some columns, he answered readers' questions, such as how small businesses might use computers, what young people should study if they want a job working with computers, and what future technology might become important. In other columns, Bill wrote about the qualities that make someone a good manager, employee, or computer programmer. Readers sent questions by e-mail to askbill@microsoft. com.

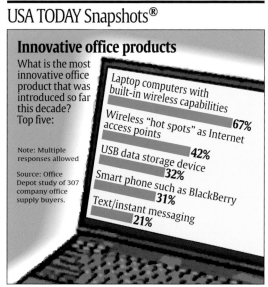

USA TODAY Snapshots®

Innovative office products

What is the most innovative office product that was introduced so far this decade? Top five:

Note: Multiple responses allowed

Source: Office Depot study of 307 company office supply buyers.

Laptop computers with built-in wireless capabilities **67%**

Wireless "hot spots" as Internet access points **42%**

USB data storage device **32%**

Smart phone such as BlackBerry **31%**

Text/instant messaging **21%**

By Jae Yang and Alejandro Gonzalez, USA TODAY, 2006

Eye on the Horizon

In November 1995, Bill published the first edition of *The Road Ahead.* In this book with an attached CD-ROM, he described the history of computing and predicted future trends. A year later, he published a revised edition, which focused more on the Internet. Both books were best-sellers in more than twenty countries. Bill donated the $3 million he earned from the sale of *The Road Ahead* to the National Foundation for the Improvement of Education. This nonprofit organization helps teachers learn to use computers and other technology in their classrooms.

All smiles: Bill did many interviews to promote Windows 95.

Bill explains in *The Road Ahead* that he has always tried to take the long view—meaning he looks far into the future and plans ahead. He tries to make decisions that will be good for his company over a long period, not just in the immediate future. But with technology changing so quickly, it is difficult to predict what will happen in the computer industry. For example, even Bill Gates nearly missed the Internet turnoff in the road of developing technology.

In the more than thirty years since personal computers were first made, they have been getting more and more powerful. They have more memory and can work faster. In *The Road Ahead*, Bill predicts that faster, more powerful computers will lead to amazing products that currently exist only in people's dreams.

Family matters: Bill and Melinda attend a news conference for the Gates Foundation. The couple would welcome their first child in 1996.

Family Man

Bill Gates had come far since 1975, when he left Harvard to follow his dream. He had started a successful company from scratch. He had become enormously rich. He had married the love of his life. What was left for him to achieve?

When he was in his twenties and early thirties, Bill hadn't wanted to be a family man. He had dated casually, not wanting to settle down. He even said that children scared him. But after Melinda came on the scene and after he became Uncle Trey to his sister's children, Bill's views gradually changed.

On April 26, 1996, Bill was at Melinda's side when she gave birth to their daughter, Jennifer Katharine Gates. Later, he made jokes to colleagues about more than business worries keeping him up at night. In his desk drawer at work, he kept a photograph of himself holding Jennifer. "I used to think I wouldn't be all that interested in the baby until she was two or so and could talk," Bill admitted. "But I'm totally into it now. She's just started to say 'ba-ba' and have a personality."

Bill's father was happy to see his son in his new role as a dad. "He just loves that little girl," said Bill Gates Sr. "It's so marvelous to see. It's very gratifying to a father to see his own son has the same feeling I had about him and his sisters. It's really gratifying."

On the business front, MSNBC, a joint project between Microsoft and the NBC television network, debuted in July 1996. The project

Joint venture: Bill *(on the big screen)* helped launch the television network MSNBC in 1996. He appears here with *(left to right)* NBC executives and personalities Robert Wright, Jane Pauley, Andrew Lack, and Brian Williams.

brought news and information to television viewers via the MSNBC channel, while Internet users could get more information on the MSNBC website. They could also read an online magazine called *Slate*.

Homecoming

Construction on Bill's house had dragged on for six years. Bill was aware that neighbors might be tired of having construction vehicles, noise, and dust nearby. So he hired work crews to mow the neighbors' lawns, do free landscaping, and wash the dust off their vehicles.

Although the house wasn't entirely completed in late 1997, the Gates family moved in. Five pavilions, connected by underground tunnels, make up the complex. One pavilion holds a grand entry hall, guest rooms, a theater, a dining room that seats 120, conference rooms, a computer room, and a library. Another pavilion contains a beach house, hot tub, and swimming pool. Another holds a caretaker's home. The family's private living space takes up two floors of the main pavilion. It includes a family room, exercise room, trampoline room, and bedrooms for children and a nanny. Parking

After waiting seven years and paying more than $54 million for his new house, Bill expected everything to work. Yet he wrote in his newspaper column about one technological bug. He had a movable television screen set up at the end of his bed. One night the screen wouldn't move down when he was done watching—it wouldn't even turn off. Instead, it glowed bright blue. Bill had to throw a blanket over it so he could go to sleep.

IN F⊕CUS

The Fast Lane

Bill loves fast cars. Over the years, he has gotten many speeding tickets. In high school, he owned an orange Mustang convertible. In the early days of Microsoft, Bill bought himself a Porsche 930 Turbo. He later added a Lexus and a Ferrari 348. Several more Porsches followed, including a Porsche 959 valued at about one million dollars.

In 1997 Bill and his close friend, Andy Evans, invested in Professional SportsCar Racing, Inc. (PSR). They bought two racetracks and tried to bring international teams into the U.S.-led sport. By December of 1997, however, PSR had been sold. But many people wonder what Bill has in store for the world of sports car racing in the future.

Car lover: The first Porsche that Bill bought was a 930 Turbo.

space for twenty cars, hidden underground, houses Bill's collection of sports cars. The informal landscaping, which includes wetlands and a trout stream, makes the house seem like a natural part of the environment.

The library is Bill's favorite room. He hired a book dealer to help choose the books. "It all goes back to the early experience that both Melinda and I had growing up with libraries in our communities," he explained.

Bill and Melinda continued to make charitable contributions. They gave $100 million to a health organization that would vaccinate children in poor countries. They contributed $200 million to the Gates Library Foundation, organized in 1995 to help libraries in the United States and Canada take advantage of computer technology. The foundation considered the needs of libraries in low-income states and poverty-stricken urban areas and gave them software and computers with Internet access. With the Internet, someone in a poor area can use the same resources as those in well-to-do neighborhoods, Bill pointed out.

Although Bill viewed the Internet as a powerful educational

Speaking out: Melinda is involved in many charities. She served as the keynote speaker at an event for Children's Hospital in Seattle in 1997.

resource, he still valued books. "It all goes back to the early experience that both Melinda and I had growing up with libraries in our communities," he explained. "I loved to check out books." He insisted that libraries not neglect their book collections just because they had computers. "Even though my house

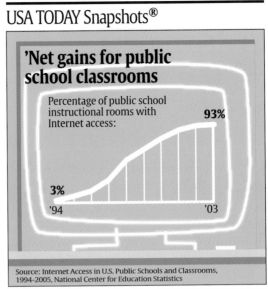

USA TODAY Snapshots®

'Net gains for public school classrooms

Percentage of public school instructional rooms with Internet access:

93%

3%

'94   '03

Source: Internet Access in U.S. Public Schools and Classrooms, 1994-2005, National Center for Education Statistics

By Tracey Wong Briggs and Sam Ward, USA TODAY, 2007

has a lot of technology, and this grant to libraries relates to technology, if you want to do something good for children, the most important thing you can do is cultivate a love of reading and to get them to be competent browsing through books and checking out books. I'm already doing that with my daughter," Bill said.

Bill tried to downplay his wealth, but he was not immune to the problems, serious or laughable, that being rich could cause. In March 1997, Bill received a frightening letter. The writer, a young man named Adam Quinn Pletcher, threatened to kill Gates if he didn't pay him $5 million. FBI agents caught the man, who was also wanted for defrauding people on the Internet. About the time Pletcher went on trial, Bill was in Belgium for business. On his way to meet with Belgian officials, Bill got a surprise. Pranksters shoved two custard pies in his face. Startled but unhurt, Bill wiped his face and glasses and went on to the meeting. He later quipped, "The worst part was that the pies were not very tasty."

June 25, 1997

Charitable gifts on the rise: Gates' $200 million donation tops '97 list

From the Pages of
USA TODAY

What does Microsoft CEO Bill Gates get for his $200 million gift to upgrade public libraries?

a) a huge tax break.

b) a chance to burnish his public image.

c) a chance to help children.

d) all of the above.

Answer: D.

Gates is not alone in discovering the benefits of giving. "It's fashionable again," says Jodie Allen, Washington editor of cyber-magazine *Slate*, which recently started a rolling list of the 60 top philanthropists. She sees Gates' personal gift as an encouraging sign of the times. "The people who have made fortunes are now starting to give back," she says.

Charitable contributions by Americans rose 7.3 percent to $150.7 billion last year, according to the American Association of Fund-Raising Counsel Trust for Philanthropy.

Already this year, "there has been an enormous number of big gifts," says Stacy Palmer, managing editor of the *Chronicle of Philanthropy*. Dean Buntrock, founder of WMX Technologies, donated $26 million to St. Olaf College. Hollywood honcho Michael Ovitz gave $25 million to the UCLA Medical Center.

But Gates has topped them all. And some critics think it was about time. In April, media mogul Ted Turner publicly called on Gates and Berkshire Hathaway's Warren Buffett—the two wealthiest men in America—to donate more.

Gates' gift—supplemented by $200 million in software from Microsoft—has raised talk of a legacy that might someday rival that of Andrew Carnegie, who championed public libraries at the turn of the century. Gates' and Microsoft's gift is about half what Carnegie's lifetime gift was in today's dollars.

Fair or not, Gates "has had a tightwad reputation," says Al Ries of marketing consultant Ries & Ries. "I think he was under some pressure to make a big gift to get some press and get over that."

No matter what his motive, public library advocates couldn't be happier.

"This is the biggest idea for libraries in 100 years," says Elizabeth Martinez, executive director of the American Library Association. "It will make the 21st century library one where everyone can learn."

Gates' contribution will be used to put computers in libraries in low-income areas. The Gates Library Foundation, which will direct the program, aims to work with more than half the 17,000 public libraries in North America. The $200 million will be granted over five years.

Gates will be able to deduct a large portion of the gift, reducing the tax burden on his annual income. His salary and bonus last year was a mere $562,588. His 282.2 million shares of Microsoft stock are worth nearly $35 billion.

Melinda and Bill

Gates' associates say his personal finances had nothing to do with his contribution. "He's passionate about this," says Patty Stonesifer, president of the foundation. She says to expect much more from Bill and his wife, Melinda. Gates ranked third in last January's *Fortune* list of the biggest givers, and looks primed to reach the top. Gates has long pledged to give away most of his money before he dies.

"This is just the beginning," Stonesifer says.

—James Kim; Christina Diaz, June 25, 1997

A Date with Congress

On March 2, 1998, Bill met Melinda in Washington, D.C. Like other tourists, they visited the Capitol and the National Gallery. They grabbed a quick pizza for dinner and went back to their hotel. Bill wanted to prepare for the next day, when he would testify about the computer industry before a committee made up of members of Congress. He finished typing up notes on his laptop computer and rehearsed aloud his five-minute speech.

Bill was part of a panel of computer company leaders who spoke at the hearing. He told the story of how Microsoft had succeeded by constantly improving its products. He pointed out that competition among computer software makers was fierce and how competition kept software prices low. He emphasized that the government should not interfere in the computer business by telling software makers how to design their products. After the hearing, Bill signed autographs and talked with reporters.

Congressional scrutiny: Bill (*far left*) testified at a U.S. Senate hearing on techology in 1998 along with heads of other U.S. software companies.

Out and about: Bill and Melinda wear formal attire to an event in New York City in 1998.

Then Bill and Melinda caught a flight to New York City. Bill had been invited to help celebrate the seventy-fifth anniversary of *Time* magazine at a fancy dinner at Radio City Music Hall. At this dinner, famous guests were to give short speeches, paying tribute to important people of the twentieth century. Bill was asked to speak about the Wright brothers, inventors of the airplane. He was a little nervous. He was used to speaking to computer specialists, not celebrities. Yet his enthusiasm for the Wright brothers came through in his talk.

The next morning, Bill visited a school in the Harlem area of New York. There, he spoke with sixth graders who were using laptop computers as a way to improve their learning skills. Then he visited the New York Public Library for a question-and-answer session with television reporter Charlie Rose.

Learning on a laptop: Bill *(second from left)* talks with students at a school in the Harlem area of New York City in 1998.

At the end of this unusually busy week, Bill was glad to get home to see Jennifer. She and Dada, as she called him, liked to play together, read books, and play with a Barney program on the computer. Around the Gates household, Bill had to be careful not to say the word *computer* around Jennifer. If he did, the two-year-old would follow him around, saying " 'puter, 'puter, 'puter," until he played a computer game with her. "I'm very lucky. My daughter is a very happy, joyful person," Bill said.

In July 1998, Bill gave a speech at a party at Microsoft headquarters to celebrate the launch of Windows 98. Until then Windows programs had been designed especially for business PC users. Windows 98 was the first operating system made particularly with home PC users in mind. Bill predicted that by the year 2001, six of every ten homes in the United States would have PCs. Of those six homes, five would have computers hooked up to the Internet. "The PC and the Internet will become as fundamental tomorrow as the automobile is today," he predicted.

Legal Battle

But Microsoft's future role in the computer industry was uncertain because more legal battles loomed on the horizon. The owners of some computer companies accused Microsoft of being a monopoly—a company that has nearly complete control of an industry. A monopoly can control the prices of the products it sells. It can charge unfairly high prices or sell products at such low prices that other companies, unable to match these prices, go out of business. Because nine out of ten new computers sold in 1998 had Microsoft's Windows 95 already installed, some people suggested that the company held a monopoly on personal computer operating systems.

In October 1998, the U.S. Justice Department and twenty states sued Microsoft, alleging that the company had been forcing computer makers to sell its Internet Explorer browser if they wanted a license to sell Windows 95. Lawyers for the Justice Department also tried to prove that Microsoft held a monopoly on operating systems and that this monopoly harmed consumers. Moreover, government lawyers accused Microsoft of using illegal practices to keep other makers of Internet browsers from competing. Their arguments were persuasive.

Though Bill Gates did not testify at the trial, government lawyers had questioned him on videotape beforehand. The lawyers then showed pieces of the videotape during the trial. Bill felt that by projecting the video on a large screen and showing his answers out of context, they portrayed him as a dictator and a villain. Others felt that Bill did run a monopolistic company that was out to crush all competitors. Reporters had a field day, speculating on the outcome of the trial and what it would mean for Microsoft and Bill.

The trial moved at a fast pace. In December the attorney general of South Carolina decided the case against Microsoft was weak and removed his state as a participant in the trial. After a two-week holiday recess, the trial resumed in January 1999.

Microsoft lawyers stated their case. They called witnesses who testified that Microsoft did not harm consumers with its products or policies. Instead, the witnesses argued, Microsoft offered computer users good products at reasonable prices. Witnesses also described the tough competition Microsoft faced—specifically from companies that made handheld computers and Internet software. In March U.S. district judge Thomas Penfield Jackson, who presided over the trial, ordered a three-month recess so that he could try another case. During the break, government lawyers held talks with Microsoft lawyers, but the two sides could not come to an out-of-court agreement. The trial resumed in June 1999. With the final witness leaving the stand on the seventy-sixth day of proceedings, Judge Jackson had mountains of documents and testimony to consider before reaching a verdict.

Order in the court: U.S. district judge Thomas Penfield Jackson presided over the case against Microsoft.

IN FOCUS

Business @ the Speed of Thought

What was Bill doing during the trial? As well as his daily work at Microsoft, he was putting the finishing touches on his new book, *Business @ the Speed of Thought*. Gates predicted that within ten years, business operations would change dramatically. Because computers make more information available to workers, the workers need to learn how to use this information to improve their companies. In his book,

Gates suggested ways for business leaders to use digital information and gave examples of how some companies are doing so already.

When the book appeared in March 1999, Gates went on tour to promote it. He gave interviews and appeared on television shows. As with his earlier book, Gates donated much of his share of the money from the sale of the book to charity.

In March 1999, Microsoft launched Internet Explorer 5.0, an improved version of the company's Web browser. Within a week, users had downloaded one million copies of the browser from the Internet.

Privately, Bill and Melinda were awaiting the birth of their second child. When Rory John Gates was born on May 23, 1999, Bill took a short leave from Microsoft. "Bill and Melinda are thrilled to be new parents once again," a Microsoft spokesperson announced. "Jennifer is very excited to have a brother." The Gates family added a third child in 2002, a girl named Phoebe Adele Gates.

Risky business: Microsoft's corporate policies under Bill's leadership were criticized by many.

Funding the Future

In November 1999, Judge Jackson ruled on the Microsoft case. He declared Microsoft to be a monopoly whose influence hurt consumers. "Microsoft has demonstrated that it will use its prodigious market power and immense profits to harm any firm that insists on pursuing initiatives that could intensify competition against one of Microsoft's core products," the judge wrote in his findings.

The judge addressed specific cases of Microsoft's attempts to harm other companies, citing its interaction with Intel, a maker of microprocessors (chips), as one example. In the mid-1990s, Intel had been working on a product that Microsoft felt would threaten Windows. Bill met with Intel CEO Andy Grove a number of times. He eventually told Grove that Microsoft would not support PCs run by Intel chips unless Intel stopped development of their own product. Needing Microsoft's support, Intel ended the project. Bill later wrote an e-mail to other Microsoft executives saying, "If Intel is not sticking totally to its part of the deal let me know."

Another example of Microsoft's influence was its agreement with Compaq, a PC company. Compaq had decided to sell its PCs with the Web browser Netscape Navigator already installed. Microsoft offered to charge Compaq a special, very low price for Windows if Compaq would agree to preinstall Microsoft's Web browser instead. Judge Jackson stated that this example revealed "the pressure that Microsoft is willing to apply to [companies] that show reluctance to cooperate."

Resolution

Bill responded to the judge's ruling by saying that the finding was only a small step in the legal process. He still planned to "win the war." In December 1999, while the media speculated about what punishment Microsoft might receive, Microsoft representatives and Justice Department lawyers met privately to work out a solution.

In November 2001, Microsoft and the Justice Department agreed on a proposed settlement designed to resolve the dispute. The settlement makes it easier for consumers to choose among various PC products. Microsoft will no longer be able to use its influence to force companies such as Compaq to sell PCs that only contain Microsoft products. Microsoft will also no longer be able to use its market dominance to manipulate companies such as Intel, which cannot survive without Microsoft's support.

The settlement agreed upon in 2001 goes a long way toward creating a fair and open market for PC consumers. But many people feel

Bill and Bill: Even while Microsoft was dealing with the recent ruling by Judge Jackson, Bill *(left)* continued to work. He attended an economic conference at the White House in Washington, D.C., with President Bill Clinton in 2000.

the settlement didn't go far enough. They think that Microsoft got off the hook too easily and should have been forced to pay for the unfair business practices of the past. Nine states complained to the court and asked that tougher penalties be imposed on Microsoft. The court, however, ruled that the settlement was in the public's interest.

Trouble Overseas

Finally, Microsoft's monopoly problems in the United States were over. But Microsoft had also been sued by the European Commission (EC, a branch of government of the European Union) for being a monopoly harmful to consumers. The EC said Microsoft has a monopoly because of its strategy of bundling, or including other pieces of software along with Windows. It said that bundling limited the choices that consumers had.

The EC focused its case on the media player that Microsoft included with every copy of Windows it sold. The media player was software that played music and movies on a computer. The commission said that including the media player with Windows limited the choice consumers had to use other media players. In March of 2004, a European court ordered Microsoft to offer a version of Windows without its media player software. Microsoft was also ordered to pay a fine of $613 million.

The ruling on software bundling applied only to Europe. But it was important because it was the first time Microsoft had been ordered to stop bundling its software products and features with Windows. Bundling is one of Microsoft's most basic and important marketing strategies. Still, Microsoft only had to offer a version of Windows without the media player. It could still offer a version of Windows that included the media player. In January of 2005, Microsoft announced it would do what the court ordered—but it planned to appeal the decision in a higher court.

Moving On

With the antitrust lawsuits in the past, Bill and Microsoft have refocused on the future. Bill's normal workday has changed greatly in the past few years. He no longer spends most of his time at work and even finds some time on weekends to relax.

At the ball game: Bill and Melinda attend a Seattle Mariners baseball game in 2000. In recent years, Bill has tried to find more free time to spend with his family.

Technology has changed the structure of Bill's workday. But he still doesn't like to waste a minute. "Time is the scarce resource and I treat it that way," Bill explains. Bill uses e-mail and an online calendar to help organize his day. E-mail is the most popular form of communication at Microsoft. Bill accepts about one hundred e-mails each day from Microsoft employees and business associates. He does his best to read and respond to every e-mail he receives.

Bill works from a single computer that is hooked up to three screens. The screen on the left contains a list of all the e-mails he has recently received. The screen in the middle shows the e-mail that Bill is currently reading or writing. On the right, the third screen displays the computer's browser, so Bill can easily search for files and save documents, among other things. This setup allows Bill to focus on the project at hand while still monitoring blogs he follows and incoming e-mails.

As technology advances at Microsoft, paper is becoming less important. Bill still reads newspapers, but he gets most of his news from online sources. When attending a meeting, Bill brings along his Tablet PC to take notes. A Tablet PC is a flat computer that looks like a notepad. It does almost everything that a desktop computer can do but is much smaller and more easily transported. With a Tablet PC, Bill can use a stylus to write notes just like on a paper notepad. Bill's days are often filled with meetings, so new, time-saving technology such as the Tablet PC is very important at Microsoft.

Even with the newest and most innovative technology at his fingertips, Bill still relies on an old-fashioned, low-tech tool while in the office. He uses a whiteboard and colored markers to share ideas with colleagues or to brainstorm on his own.

Past and present: Bill is shown holding a touch-screen portable computer, a recent Microsoft product. In front is an Altair 8800, the first personal computer.

Every year, Bill and other top employees take a weeklong retreat from the office. Bills calls this time Think Week, and that's what the participants do. They do research, think, and talk about what the future might hold. They talk about what role Microsoft might play in the future. Think Week participants used to take notes and exchange ideas on paper. Technology such as the Tablet PC allows the entire process to be digital, so the ideas generated during Think Week can be shared with the whole company.

IN FOCUS

Gaming for Profit

New ideas and technological innovations are at the heart of what Microsoft does. One of Microsoft's newest products is the Xbox 360 video game console. The Xbox 360 was an immediate hit with consumers when it hit stores in 2005. With a sleek new design, loads of fun games, and the most potent processing power in the console industry, the Xbox 360 is a major force with video game fans around the world. With other new products such as Windows Vista and the Zune multimedia player, Microsoft remains on the cutting edge of new technology.

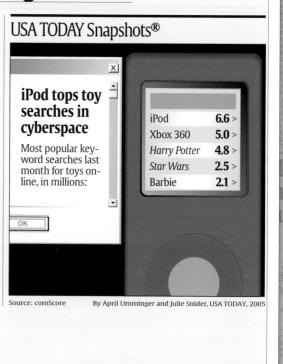

USA TODAY Snapshots®

iPod tops toy searches in cyberspace

Most popular keyword searches last month for toys online, in millions:

iPod	6.6 >
Xbox 360	5.0 >
Harry Potter	4.8 >
Star Wars	2.5 >
Barbie	2.1 >

Source: comScore   By April Umminger and Julie Snider, USA TODAY, 2005

Evolving Priorities

While Bill is still as enthusiastic as ever about Microsoft and the computer industry, other concerns and responsibilities have cut into the time he spends in the office. In an interview in 2006, Bill said, "I believe that with great wealth comes great responsibility, a responsibility to give back to society, a responsibility to see that those resources are put to work in the best possible way to help those most in need." To fulfill this responsibility, Bill and his wife created the

Bill & Melinda Gates Foundation. Formed in 2000, the Bill & Melinda Gates Foundation strives to address health and education issues around the world. The foundation is organized into three programs. The Global Development program helps millions of people in the developing world with agricultural, financial, and library projects. The Global Health program fights the AIDS epidemic and other diseases such as tuberculosis and malaria in developing countries. The U.S. program focuses on funding education programs and library initiatives that benefit vulnerable people in the United States.

Foundation focus: Members of the media look on as Bill attends computer class with a student at a high school in Miami, Florida. The Bill & Melinda Gates Foundation has granted money to schools throughout the United States for computer labs, libraries, and other purposes.

Foundation donation: *(Left to right)* Bill, Melinda, and Warren Buffett at a news conference in 2006 to announce Buffett's planned donation to the Gates Foundation.

Funding such ambitious projects is a major challenge, even for one of the world's richest people. When Warren Buffett, CEO of Berkshire Hathaway and Bill's friend, pledged to donate much of his vast fortune to the Bill & Melinda Gates Foundation in 2006, it was a huge boon

Warren Buffett is not the only person who admires the philanthropic work of the Bill & Melinda Gates Foundation. Along with Bono, lead singer of the rock band U2, *Time* magazine named Bill and Melinda Gates "Persons of the Year" for 2005. The Gateses were noted for their efforts to eliminate disease and improve the lives of people around the world. Bono was honored in part as cofounder of DATA, which stands for "Debt, AIDS, Trade, Africa." DATA works to eradicate AIDS and poverty in developing countries.

for the charity. Buffett plans to donate most of his enormous fortune to various charities over the course of a few years. Of that donation, Buffett plans to give the majority of the money to the Bill & Melinda Gates Foundation. Buffett wrote of the gift, "I greatly admire what the Bill & Melinda Gates Foundation is accomplishing and want to materially expand its future capabilities."

Bill's focus on his foundation is causing big changes at Microsoft. At a news conference in 2006, Bill announced, "Today I am working full-time for Microsoft and part-time for the Gates Foundation. Starting two years from now, I will shift, work full-time at the Foundation, part-time at Microsoft as Chairman and as a senior technical adviser." Bill will continue to have important responsibilities at Microsoft, but he will leave the day-to-day operation of the company to trusted employees such as Steve Ballmer and Ray Ozzie.

Microsoft management: Bill *(left)* looks on as Steve Ballmer speaks at the launch party for Windows Vista in 2007.

Looking Forward

While Bill transitions into his new roles, Microsoft continues to look for ways to expand and stay ahead of fierce industry competition. The company has found that sometimes the best opportunities for growth come from external sources. In October 2007, Microsoft paid $240 million for stock in the online social network Facebook. Although they

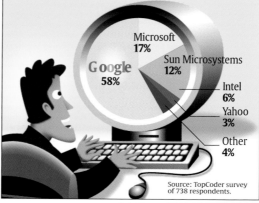

USA TODAY Snapshots®

Programmers' favorite: Google

Companies where computer programmers would work if compensation were not a factor:

Google 58%
Microsoft 17%
Sun Microsystems 12%
Intel 6%
Yahoo 3%
Other 4%

Source: TopCoder survey of 738 respondents.

By Jae Yang and Bob Laird, USA TODAY, 2005

IN FOCUS

Facebook

The people who work at Facebook refer to their website as a "social utility" where people can meet, network, share, and play. Founded in 2004 in Palo Alto, California, the company is growing very quickly and recently launched a Spanish-language site.

Facebook is unique because it allows people to create their own applications to use on the site, which are known as third-party software. Third-party software applications on Facebook include games of many kinds and new ways to share music and photographs. With about 60 million members, most of whom check the site often, Facebook has a bright future.

only acquired a 1.6 percent stake in Facebook for such a vast sum of money, Microsoft officials feel it was a worthwhile investment in one of the Internet's most popular sites. An even bigger deal was on the horizon as Microsoft attempted to acquire the Internet search engine company Yahoo! for an astonishing $47.5 billion in 2008. After months of negotiations, however, the two sides could not agree on a sale price and the deal was canceled.

As Microsoft looks for ways to grow its market share, the Bill & Melinda Gates Foundation is expanding its charitable giving. The foundation grants money to fight many of the world's problems in a variety of unique ways. To help prevent future outbreaks of malaria, the foundation has granted money to organizations in Africa, Seattle, London, and many places in between. The money is intended to strengthen existing malaria programs as well as provide funding for new research.

When *Forbes* magazine released its list of the world's richest people in March of 2008, there was a big change at the top. Bill Gates was no longer number one. Instead, Bill's friend and philanthropic partner Warren Buffett led the group with a fortune estimated at $62 billion. Until 2008 Bill had been listed as the wealthiest person in the world for thirteen years in a row.

One of the more unique ventures that receives support from the foundation is the AIDS JaaGO project, which created four short films by respected Indian directors. The films are available for viewing through the Bill & Melinda Gates Foundation website. The purpose of the films is to increase awareness of the AIDS problem, as well as to destroy some of the myths linked to the disease.

January 25, 2008

Microsoft revenue hits record at $16.4B

<u>From the Pages of</u>
<u>USA TODAY</u>

What recession?

Microsoft on Thursday reported record quarterly revenue—and a 79% pop in profits. And it raised its fiscal-year outlook, signaling a belief that tech spending will persist at a healthy clip.

"We're seeing strong growth internationally and decent growth in the U.S.," says Frank Brod, Microsoft's chief accounting officer.

Microsoft shares rose 5% in after-hours trading to $34.80.

For its fiscal second quarter, Microsoft reported revenue of $16.4 billion, a quarterly record, and net income of $4.7 billion, or 50 cents a share. That's up from revenue of $12.5 billion and net income of $2.6 billion, or 26 cents, the same period a year earlier. It sold more than 100 million Vista licenses. Revenue in its entertainment unit, which includes Xbox, Windows Mobile and Zune, rose 3 percent.

Those strong results allowed the company to raise its outlook for the fiscal year, which ends June 30. Microsoft said it now expects earnings of $1.85 to $1.88 a share for the year, and revenue of $59.9 billion to $60.5 billion. Analysts had previously estimated $1.81 a share and revenue of $59.36 billion for 2008.

"If you look at earnings from IBM, Microsoft and other big tech (supplier) companies, most of them seem to have OK numbers and OK outlooks," says Sid Parakh, tech stocks analyst at McAdams Wright Ragen. "That bodes well, at least from a tech-spending perspective."

Meanwhile, Microsoft Chairman Bill Gates called for a new "creative capitalism" to help the world's poorest people. At the World Economic Forum in Davos, Switzerland, Gates urged business leaders and politicians "to find a way to make the aspects of capitalism that serve wealthier people serve poorer people as well." Gates said he wants to see the benefits of science and technology reach the poor.

—Byron Acohido, January 25, 2008

Another of the foundation's many health ventures in 2008 was a $19 million donation to the Drugs for Neglected Diseases Initiative to help find a cure for African sleeping sickness. African sleeping sickness is caused by a parasite and can lead to a long list of symptoms, including death. Also in 2008, at the World Economic Forum in Davos, Switzerland, Gates made the announcement that his foundation would donate $306 million to help farmers in developing countries. The money is to be used for ventures such as teaching people helpful agricultural practices, advising farmers about how best to get their products to market, and improving soil quality for millions of people.

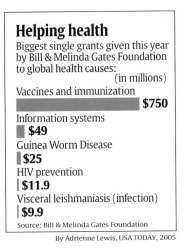

Helping health

Biggest single grants given this year by Bill & Melinda Gates Foundation to global health causes:
(in millions)

Vaccines and immunization
$750

Information systems
$49

Guinea Worm Disease
$25

HIV prevention
$11.9

Visceral leishmaniasis (infection)
$9.9

Source: Bill & Melinda Gates Foundation

By Adrienne Lewis, USA TODAY, 2005

Through the unprecedented success of his company, Bill Gates and the foundation he and his wife created have a chance to make an incredible impact on the world. The influence of the foundation is already felt far and wide, and much more could be accomplished in the years to come. But as Bill said in a recent speech, the challenges are great: "Imagine, just for the sake of discussion, that you had a few hours a week and a few dollars a month to donate to a cause— and you wanted to spend that time and money where it would have the greatest impact in saving and improving lives. Where would you spend it? For Melinda and for me, the challenge is the same: how can we do the most good for the greatest number with the resources we have."

Though Microsoft and Bill have faced challenges over the years, few people would dispute Bill Gates's importance to the world. He has helped create a technological revolution. He is making the

Man with a mission: Bill waves to reporters as he leaves a meeting in Paris, France, in 2008.

world a better place through his generous spirit and commitment to giving. When historians look back on the life and accomplishments of Bill Gates, they will undoubtedly rank him as one of the most influential people of our time.

GLOSSARY

bug: a flaw in a computer program

CD-ROM: compact disc with read-only memory; a compact disc containing graphics, sound, text, or other data that can be read by a computer

chip: an integrated circuit; a tiny piece of silicon holding the network of electronic components that form the "brains" of a computer

code: a set of instructions for a computer

digital: information stored as numbers

download: to transfer data from a computer or the Internet to another computer

graphical user interface (GUI): a computer program that allows a user to interact easily with the computer, typically by using a mouse to make choices from menus or groups of icons

hardware: the physical components of a computer

hypertext markup language (HTML): a computer language used to create Web pages

icon: a graphic symbol on a computer screen that represents an application, file, or command

language: a system of computer communication with specific rules and vocabulary

mainframe computer: a large, powerful computer used by a business or institution to perform multiple tasks

operating system: software that controls the primary operations of a computer and directs the processing of programs

PC: personal computer; a small desktop computer designed to be used by a single person

program: coded instructions for running a specific computer operation

software: the programs and procedures associated with a computer system

spreadsheet: a computer accounting program

stylus: a small, pointed tool used on pressure-sensitive computer screens

Teletype: a machine used to communicate, via telephone lines, with a mainframe computer

Web: the World Wide Web; the global network of Internet sites and pages

word processing: the creation and editing of documents on a computer

WYSIWYG: "What You See Is What You Get"; a computer display that exactly reflects the printed document

FURTHER READING AND WEBSITES

Books

Firestone, Mary. *Wireless Technology*. Minneapolis: Lerner Publications Company, 2009.

O'Connor, Barbara. *Leonardo da Vinci: Renaissance Genius*. Minneapolis: Twenty-First Century Books, 2003.

Peters, Craig. *Bill Gates: Software Genius of Microsoft*. Berkeley Heights, NJ: Enslow Publishers, 2003.

Sherman, Josepha. *The History of the Personal Computer*. New York: Franklin Watts, 2003.

Woods, Michael and Mary B. *Ancient Computing: From Counting to Calendars*. Minneapolis: Twenty-First Century Books, 2000.

Websites

Bill & Melinda Gates Foundation
http://www.gatesfoundation.org
The official foundation site includes articles about current national and international issues, the history of the foundation, information about seeking grants, and also a description of past grants given to other programs and organizations.

Bill Gates' Website
http://www.microsoft.com/presspass/exec/billg/default.mspx
Part of the Microsoft website, this page contains a brief biography on Bill Gates as well as links to his speeches and published writings.

SOURCE NOTES

9   Bill Gates, Nathan Myrvold, and Peter Rinearson, *The Road Ahead* (New York: Viking, 1995), 172.

9   Stephen Manes and Paul Andrews, *Gates: How Microsoft's Mogul Reinvented an Industry—and Made Himself the Richest Man in America* (New York: Doubleday, 1993), 16.

10   Walter Isaacson, "In Search of the Real Bill Gates," *Time*, January 13, 1997, 47.

12   Manes and Andrews, 24.

12   Isaacson, 47.

15–16   Gates, 1.

17   Isaacson, 48.

17   Gates, 18.

18   Ibid.

19   Ibid.

20   Ibid., 290–91.

23   Isaacson, 48.

39   James Wallace and Jim Erickson, *Hard Drive: Bill Gates and the Making of the Microsoft Empire* (New York: John Wiley and Sons, 1992), 250.

41   Brent Schlender, "What Bill Gates Really Wants," *Fortune*, January 16, 1995, n. p.

47   Manes and Andrews, 342.

51   Gates, 327.

51   Bill Gates, "The Fascinating Interplay of Biotechnology and Computers," *Microsoft*, http://www.microsoft.com (October 21, 1997).

53   Alan Deutschman, "Bill Gates' Next Challenge," *Fortune*, December 28, 1992, 35.

54   Gates, 327.

58   Biography "Bill Gates," VHS, ABC News Production and A & E Television Network, 1998.

62   David Ellis, "Love Bytes: Computer Whiz Bill Gates Ends His Reign as America's Richest Bachelor," *People Weekly*, January 17, 1994, n. p.

65   Microsoft, "The William H. Gates Foundation," *Microsoft*, http://www.microsoft.com (September 3, 1998).

66   Gates, 1.

67   Bill Gates, "Ask Bill," *Microsoft*, http://www.microsoft.com (January 17, 1995).

69   Bill Gates, "The Future of Communications," *Microsoft*, http://www .microsoft.com (n. d.).

69   Michael J. Miller, "Interview: Bill Gates, Microsoft," *PC Magazine*, March 25, 1997, 233.

70   Brent Schlender, "Whose Internet Is It Anyway?" *Fortune*, December 11, 1995, 126.

77   Isaacson, 51.

77   Biography "Bill Gates."

81   Leonard Kniffel, "Gates Expands Access Mission during Alabama Visit," *American Libraries*, April 1998, n. p.

81   Evan St. Lifer, "Gates Speaks to Libraries," *Library Journal*, July 1997, 45.

81   Jean Seligman, "Now an Anti-trust Violation?" *Newsweek*, February 16, 1998, 64.

86   *U.S. News and World Report*, "Chairman Gates, Up Close and Personal," October 19, 1998, 15.

87   Microsoft, "Microsoft CEO Bill Gates Sees PC in 60 Percent of U.S. Homes in 2001," press release, http://www.microsoft.com (July 29, 1998).

90   Thomas Penfield Jackson, "Microsoft Antitrust Trial Findings of Fact," *Findlaw Library*, November 5, 1999, http://www.news.findlaw.com/ microsoft.html (January 5, 2000).

91   Ibid.

94   Bill Gates, "Column," *Microsoft*, http://www.microsoft.com (August 27, 1997).

96   Bill Gates, "A New Era of Technical Leadership at Microsoft," *Microsoft*, June 15, 2006, http://www.microsoft.com/billgates/speeches/2006/06-15transition.aspx (October 30, 2006).

99   Warren Buffett, memo to Bill & Melinda Gates Foundation, *Berkshire Hathaway*, June 26, 2006, http://www.berkshirehathaway.com/donate/ bmgfltr.pdf (October 30, 2006).

99   Bill Gates, "A New Era of Technical Leadership at Microsoft."

103 Bill Gates, "Remarks of Bill Gates—Harvard Commencement," *Harvard University Gazette*, June 7, 2007, speech, http://www.news .harvard.edu/gazette/2007/06.14/99-gates.html (June 7, 2007).

SELECTED BIBLIOGRAPHY

Bill & Melinda Gates Foundation, http://www.gatesfoundation.org (May 14, 2008).

Gates, Bill. *Business @ the Speed of Thought*. New York: Warner Books, 1999.

Gates, Bill, Nathan Myrvold and Peter Rinearson. *The Road Ahead*. New York: Viking, 1995.

Ichbiah, Daniel, and Susan L. Knepper. *The Making of Microsoft*. Rocklin, CA: Prima Publishing, 1991.

Isaacson, Walter. "In Search of the Real Bill Gates." *Time*, January 13, 1997, 44–56.

Jackson, Thomas Penfield. "Microsoft Antitrust Trial Findings of Fact," *Findlaw Library*, November 5, 1999, http://news.findlaw.com/microsoft .html (January 5, 2000).

Lowe, Janet. *Bill Gates Speaks*. New York: John Wiley and Sons, 1998.

Manes, Stephen, and Paul Andrews. *Gates: How Microsoft's Mogul Reinvented an Industry—and Made Himself the Richest Man in America*. New York: Doubleday, 1993.

Microsoft. "Bill Gates, Chairman, Microsoft Corp.," *Microsoft*, July 30, 2007, http://www.microsoft.com/presspass/exec/billg/bio.mspx (May 14, 2008).

Miller, Michael J. "Interview: Bill Gates, Microsoft." *PC Magazine*, March 25, 1997, 230–234.

Wallace, James. *Overdrive: Bill Gates and the Race to Control Cyberspace*. New York: John Wiley and Sons, 1997.

Wallace, James, and Jim Erickson. *Hard Drive: Bill Gates and the Making of the Microsoft Empire*. New York: John Wiley and Sons, 1992.

INDEX

PHOTO ACKNOWLEDGMENTS

The images in this book are used with the permission of: AP Photo/Peter Dejong, p. 4; © Fred Prouser/Reuters/CORBIS, p. 5; © Popperfoto/Getty Images, p. 7; Seattle Post-Intelligencer, pp. 8, 9, 30, 35, 60; © iStockphoto .com/Hafizov Ivan, pp. 11, 26, 45, 54, 63, 82, 102; © John Dominis/Time Life Pictures/Getty Images, p. 14; © Ed Eckstein/CORBIS, p. 15; © Microsoft Corp., pp. 16, 24, 28, 37, 42; AP Photo/J. Walter Green, p. 22; AP Photo/Mike Derer, p. 23; © Albuquerque Police Dept./ZUMA Press, p. 31; AP Photo, p. 32; © Doug Wilson/CORBIS, pp. 34, 36, 38, 41, 46; © Roger Ressmeyer/CORBIS, p. 40; © Dan Lamont/CORBIS, p. 43; AP Photo/Gary Stewart, p. 48; © Oistin Macbride/CORBIS, p. 49; © Carol Halebian/Liaison/Getty Images, p. 50; © Rob Kinmonth/Time Life Pictures/Getty Images, p. 52; REUTERS/Anthony Bolante, pp. 55, 93; © Albert Ferreira/Globe Photos, Inc., p. 57; AP Photo/FILE/Lennox McLendon, p. 59; AP Photo/Dave Weaver, p. 61; REUTERS/Jeff Christensen, pp. 65, 86; © Ann Summa/Time Life Pictures/Getty Images, p. 66; © Art Resource, NY, p. 67; REUTERS/Clay Mclachlan, p. 70; © Therese Frare/AFP/ Getty Images, p. 71; © Stephen Rose/Getty Images, p. 73; © Reuters/CORBIS, p. 76; AP Photo/Wally Santana, p. 77; © Artemis Images , p. 79; AP Photo/ Barry Sweet, p. 80; © Victor Malafronte/Hulton Archive/Getty Images, p. 85; REUTERS/Colin Braley, p. 97; AP Photo/Seth Wenig, p. 98; AP Photo/Remy de la Mauviniere, file, p. 104.

ABOUT THE AUTHOR

Jeanne M. Lesinski lives in Michigan and works as a writer and editor for book and magazine publishers all over the country. She has written hundreds of factual sketches for reference books. She enjoys gardening and surfing the net.